CHOOSE LIFE:

EWAN McGREGOR AND THE BRITISH FILM REVIVAL

BY XAN BROOKS

CHAMELEON

First published in 1998 by Chameleon Books, an imprint of
André Deutsch Limited
76 Dean Street
London W1V 5HA
www.vci.co.uk

André Deutsch Limited is a subsidiary of VCI plc

A catalogue record for this book is available from the British Library

ISBN 0 233 99410 6

Cover images courtesy of PolyGram/Pictorial Press
(left and centre) and Channel 4 (right)

Typeset by Derek Doyle & Associates
Mold, Flintshire.
Printed by
MPG Books, Bodmin, Cornwall

CHOOSE LIFE

CONTENTS

ACKNOWLEDGEMENTS

In compiling this book, I relied heavily on interviews with a variety of subjects. These included Danny Boyle, Kerry Fox, Peter Greenaway, Todd Haynes, Mark Herman, Samuel L Jackson, Neil Jordan, Mike Leigh, Ken Loach, Andrew Macdonald, Irvine Welsh, plus two interviews with Ewan McGregor, whose decision not to be specifically involved with this book was respected.

I am also indebted to the following publications for source material: The *Big Issue*, the *Daily Record, Elle, Empire, Eva*, the *Daily Express*, the *Face, Film Review*, the *Guardian, Hansard, iD, Interview,* the *Independent*, the *Independent on Sunday,* the *List*, the *Daily Mail*, the *Mail on Sunday*, the *Mirror, Neon*, the *Observer, Premiere, Preview*, the *Radio Times, Scotland on Sunday*, the *Scotsman, Sight and Sound*, the *Sun*, the *Sunday Times, Time Out, The Times, Variety* and *Village Voice*.

You stagger out of a book full of dumb gratitude for the people who put up with you during the time you were writing it. Thanks, then, to Charlotte for her endless tolerance during the occasional panic attack and numerous lost weekends. Thanks, also to the indispensable BFI and to all at the *Big Issue* for their support and patience when my energies were directed elsewhere. Most of all, thank you to André Deutsch editor Anna Kiernan. Anna nurtured this project from the start, kept her head in the crises and was on hand with clear-sighted advice throughout. The book couldn't have happened without her.

PREFACE

The immediate question of course is why Ewan McGregor? Why write a book about an actor still in his twenties and, in all probability, just completing the first quarter of his career? On the face of it, this looks a valid point. Actors either dead or in their dotage inevitably provide more meat for the biographer. Their histories are behind them. McGregor's, by contrast, is being defined and re-defined by the day.

Yet McGregor matters. For a start, he can already look back on a career that actors fifty years his senior would regard with envy. He has developed his craft from low-budget British films to major league projects such as George Lucas's forthcoming *Star Wars* prequel. He has shown skill and diversity in a wide spectrum of work, from Peter Greenaway's arthouse teaser *The Pillow Book* via the pit-closure saga *Brassed Off* to Todd Haynes's layered glam-rock odyssey, *Velvet Goldmine*. He has arguably become one of the most significant actors of his generation.

Central to McGregor's status is *Trainspotting*. It was both the role which made him a star and the film credited with re-energizing a dormant industry. Its attendant hype aside, *Trainspotting* detonated like dynamite throughout the cosy world of home-grown cinema. After years of false dawns, bungled ambitions and creeping conservatism, here, one felt, was a story that spoke to modern British culture, and an actor who brought that tale to life. Those prematurely mourning the death of British cinema heaved an almost audible sigh of relief.

Trainspotting, too, is the picture which cemented McGregor's relationship with Figment Film's team of director Danny Boyle, producer Andrew Macdonald and writer John Hodge. With *Shallow Grave*, *Trainspotting* and *A Life Less Ordinary*, McGregor has become inextricably bound up with this unique trio. His rise has paralleled their rise and, for Danny Boyle, McGregor is 'the fourth musketeer': the D'Artagnan to Hodge's, Macdonald's and Boyle's core trio. He has become the face, the voice and the embodiment of the most vital production team currently at work within the British film industry.

But success has taken McGregor outside of himself, broken him out beyond the parameters of his medium. Through talent, luck, even an accident of birth, he has become a part of something bigger, the symbol of some wider cultural trend. As with Oasis, or the forerunners of Brit-art and Brit-lit, his work speaks of and to our society. Stardom has hooked him into youth culture and turned him into a point of identification; the patron saint of a creative groundswell in Britain, the influence of which continues to impact on the world at large.

COMING OF AGE

1. COMING OF AGE

'I've felt like a movie star since I was five,' Ewan McGregor once remarked. 'It just took me a while to get there.'

Time, though, is elastic. What Ewan McGregor might see as a rigorous apprenticeship would no doubt strike others as an ascent in an eye-blink. Most actors drift through years of obscurity; peppering their days on the dole with a few unrewarding bit-parts to beef up their show-reels. By contrast, McGregor's rise has been shockingly smooth. Asked recently how much time he had spent as a 'resting' actor, he was unable to stretch the period beyond four months (coming in a block after finishing on the set of *Lipstick on Your Collar*). 'I have been very lucky,' he said with a shrug in one interview.

The Ewan McGregor recipe for success looks absurdly simple. He enjoyed a comfortable upbringing with loving parents (his mum and dad were both teachers), plenty of open-air childhood pranks and a healthy disregard for formal education. He was born on the last day of March, 1971, and his first memory is of dropping his Fry's chocolate bar into the waters of his local river; standing on the bridge and bawling disconsolately at its loss. As an example of childhood trauma it registers pretty low on the Richter scale.

One suspects that Crieff made the ideal nursery slope for Ewan McGregor. It is a safe, affluent Perthshire market-town dominated at the centre by its looming Hydro hotel – a remnant from its days as a Victorian spa resort. In later years, McGregor would wax lyrical about the classic Frank Capra heartwarmer *It's a Wonderful Life*, played out in the archetypal small-town-USA environment of Bedford Falls. Capra's town was solid, provincial and resolutely unglamorous. You could sink into its cosy surrounds, but after a while its sheer never-changing familiarity began to drive you crazy. Parallels, perhaps, with 1970s Crieff. 'I liked it, and my family had roots there. But I always knew that someday I'd have to get out,' McGregor confesses. 'Too many tweedy farmers.' Growing out of Crieff was to become the key journey in the life of the young Ewan McGregor.

He took his first tottering steps at six, when he played the role of David in a church production of *David and Goliath*. This was a starchy, purist affair. The local minister, the Reverend Henry Tait, had lifted most of the dialogue whole-sale from the Bible and his hapless charges fluffed and forgot their lines with abandon. Ewan, however, benefited from diligent home coaching from his mother, and showed up word perfect on the day. 'Most children of that age have to be prodded, pushed or coached before they'll do a thing half right,' recalled the reverend years later. 'This child had natural flair.' Lest one suspect that this is just revisionism run riot, Tait presents more telling evidence. Following the show, the minister penned a short critique of *David and Goliath* in his diary. 'It was a ragged affair,' he wrote, but 'wee Ewan McGregor was outstandingly good, however, as David.' Even in infancy, it seems, 'wee Ewan' had mastered the knack of emerging from a shaky production still smelling of roses. Compare Henry Tait's review with critics' verdicts on *A Life Less Ordinary* (McGregor's sloppy, sporadically charming road movie, made some twenty years later) and the basic sentiment isn't that different.

Three weeks after his *David and Goliath* debut came another key chapter in Ewan McGregor's apprenticeship. His first trip to the Perth Odeon cinema, accompanied by his mother Carol and elder brother Colin, was to see that summer's blockbuster – an epic sci-fi fantasy set 'a long time ago in a galaxy far, far away'. Carol McGregor remembers the trip, and its aftermath: 'The boys just loved it. They both had toy light-sabres and they used them a lot at home.' For the McGregors there was a also a faint family connection here. Carol's younger brother, actor Denis Lawson, had a bit-part in *Star Wars* playing Wedge, a heroic X-Wing fighter pilot. Ewan would come to idolize the man. 'He was like something from another planet himself. He had flares on and sideboards and beads and a big sheepskin waistcoat and didn't wear any shoes. I used to think: "Shit, I want to be like *that.*"'

Throughout his childhood, McGregor came to see Lawson as the bridge into another world. The artistic success of someone from within his own family showed that Ewan's movie-star fantasies were an achievable ambition. In the meantime, in his own modest way, he began to follow suit, acting in various school productions and regailing his family with Elvis impersonations; hair slicked back, hips a-waggling. 'It became my dinner-party routine. I'd do Elvis for the grown-ups and then they'd pack me off to bed.'

McGregor was a typical seventies pop-kid. In the summer of 1977 he was a *Star Wars* groupy, twelve months on he'd jumped ship to *Grease*. The John Travolta/Olivia Newton-John musical was the big summer sensation of 1978, and provided the touchstone for numerous playground karaokes. 'I made a mean Olivia Newton-John,' Ewan recalls. 'You know, getting in touch with my feminine side.' Meantime Crieff continued to nurture him – occasionally in ways he didn't appreciate. 'I didn't hate school,' reflects McGregor. 'I just never got into it.'

School was the fee-paying Morrison's Academy. On the surface this may seem an extravagant gesture, since the McGregors hailed from a cramped bungalow on Sauchie Terrace, in one of the (comparatively) poorer parts of town. But the family's relationship with Morrison's went way back. Ewan's great-grandfather – a stonemason – had helped lay the school's foundations. His parents Jim and Carol had met and started going out together while pupils there and Jim eventually took a job as the school's PE master (nicknamed 'Wee Jim'). Ewan sang in the choir, thumped drums and played the French horn in the school band. It was this skill which brought him his first screen appearance: piping his way through a Mozart piece on Grampian TV. It was not an auspicious beginning. In an effort to 'look cool', to debunk the whole stuffy affair, McGregor kept breaking off from playing to wipe snot extravagantly from his nose. 'They had to keep cutting away to the pianist,' he remembers.

Overall, though, McGregor found his energies stifled at Morrison's. His spelling was eccentric and maths was his *bête noire*. He was happier outside the classroom. The picture that emerges of these times is of a carefree, mischief-making pastoral in the *Just William* mould. '[Crieff] was really green,' McGregor explains.

> I used to rampage around forests, and there was a big hill that we used to kick around on called the Knock. So if I think about my childhood I think about that: kicking around forests and riding horses and stuff like that. Kind of lads' stuff, because in the countryside you kind of run around in packs.

He and his mates built survivalist-style camps in the woods and bombarded any stray passers-by (ambling pensioners, pony-trekkers and the like) with fir cones, delivered at some speed from a Black Widow catapult. Later, the gang graduated to that obligatory teenage pastime: fun with fireworks. 'We'd lie them on the ground and light them,' recalls childhood friend Malcolm Copland, 'and they would shoot along the ground towards a group of people ahead.' It was, admits Ewan, 'childish nonsense. Stupid, really.'

But the youthful Ewan found himself torn between impish *joie de vivre* and high-minded saintliness. For a short spell, religion threatened to dominate his life. Although his parents were cheerfully agnostic, their son attended Sunday school and moseyed off on several Christian outward bound courses. When not clowning around in class he would turn cloyingly pious; lecturing the school trouble-makers on the teachings of Jesus. But it was a short-lived fad. 'I look back on it with slight disgust. Puberty is a confusing time, and [the Church] sank their talons into young flesh and got me.' The scales fell from his eyes one night at a church lecture on the evils of sex, when the boy looked up and saw that the chief speaker was a quick-with-his-fists local who regularly beat up his own offspring. 'And I just saw right through it,' Ewan recalls. And that was that.

By all accounts, Ewan was a popular kid; both a charmer and a clown. He'd fool around in class, but the teachers liked him too much to mete out much in the way of punishment (a few cross-country runs, the odd litter collection or the occasional ticking-off from his dad). Some schoolmates, though, argue that in terms of town status, Ewan was forever dwarfed by his elder brother, Colin: a golden boy on the sportsfield and the school captain at Morrison's Academy. Ewan could hardly help but pale by comparison. He was an adequate rugby player but was below-par at football. In terms of sport, strangely it was only golf that held any interest for him and even that played second fiddle to his real obsession; namely film. Most Saturdays, when the other lads were out kicking a ball about, Ewan would be lounging in the sitting room ogling black-and-white Hollywood movies on BBC2. His idols were Jimmy Stewart, Clark Gable and Cary Grant. This, one suspects, was his real education.

The fraternal relationship with Colin McGregor may explain Ewan's social rambunctiousness, his ceaseless quest for peer-group approval and his general lack of discrimination.

> I just wanted everybody to like me. I'd kick about with one clique, then hop over to another. And all the time I was going: "Please like me, please laugh at my jokes. Oh, go on – please." Typical fucking actor. Totally fucking insecure.

Whatever his motives, the tactic seemed to pay off. According to Fergus Adams, a pal on the outer rim of McGregor's circle, Ewan 'was always a good laugh. Some people used to think his dreams of being an actor were just a fantasy, but it didn't turn out that way.' Carol McGregor remembers that the girls, in particular, were always drawn to her son. Former classmate Ian King supports this claim: 'I think if you had to pick someone the girls were fighting over it would have to be Ewan.' One temporary victor in this battle was Vicky McNally, who went out with Ewan for a month or two during the fifth year. 'We used to write each other letters rather than doing the schoolwork,' she said, 'and these would get handed over at breaktime.' But the affair floundered when boyfriend caught girlfriend taking a few experimental tokes on a cigarette. By this point Ewan was already a practised Marlboro Man himself, yet the prospect of Vicky following suit somehow did not appeal. McGregor, schoolmates remember, flew into a major hissy-fit, and the short-lived liaison was effectively over. Girls aside, spare time was divided between the bar of a local hotel (a popular haunt for underage drinkers) and playing drums in his makeshift rock-band, Scarlet Pride. Ewan would tug on red-and-black drain-pipes, gell his hair into points, then roar his way through boisterous Billy Idol covers (such mid-eighties goth-punk staples as 'Rebel Yell' and 'White Wedding').

In 1987 McGregor reached escape velocity. School was getting him down and Crieff had grown too cramped to accommodate him. Highers were looming ominously on the horizon and McGregor wanted out.

> I was sixteen and suffering from depression. I went off the rails and kept getting brought up before the headmaster. I wasn't exactly rebellious, but inside I knew something wasn't right with my life.

After several heart-to-hearts with his parents, they agreed to let him go. Ewan's own recollection of the breakthrough conversation places it against a fittingly dramatic backdrop: a stormy February night with rain lashing at the windscreen. The family were driving from Crieff to their new home; a large house set in the countryside about ten miles beyond town. 'We felt it had come to the point where he'd stopped getting anything out of school any more,' says Carol. 'It was time we let him do what he wanted to do and see for himself whether he could make it or not.'

In cosy Crieff, small-town life rolled on without him. Best mate Malcolm Copland stayed on at Morrison's and now lives and works in Crieff as a sales manager. Fergus Adams is a civil engineer, and Vicky McNally is now Vicky Grant. a bank clerk who managed to rebound unharmed from that tumultuous fifth-form fling. Colin McGregor, too, took off on a divergent path to his younger brother. He now flies Tornado jets for the RAF. 'He gets a big kick out of what I do,' says Ewan. 'He goes to see all the films I'm in, and whenever I see a jet pass by overhead I look up and think: "Ah, that's probably my brother up there." ' On one occasion Colin took his younger brother up with him. Ewan was sick out of the window.

Spying clues to McGregor's subsequent success in these formative years is a haphazard and ultimately fruitless enterprise. This was a life most humdrum – a typical round of childhood games, grinding schooldays, fleeting girlfriends and underage drinking sprees. A life, in other words, no different from millions of others. Even his attraction to Hollywood movies and his vague showbusiness leanings (school productions, rock-star posturing) are hardly out of the ordinary. It's common practice for kids to fantasize about being Mick Jagger, Luke Skywalker, or whoever's the 'next big thing' at some stage of their development before eventually buckling down to the demands of grey reality. There was nothing of the child prodigy about Ewan McGregor. He exhibited no real prima-donna behaviour, nor tell-tale signs of obsessive genius. He was a popular lad, a quick-witted companion, a handsome and charming teenager, but was easily distracted at school and so judged to be below normal academic ability.

In retrospect, of course, it's tempting to argue that McGregor was merely keeping his powder dry during these years; biding his time until the world was ready. But this doesn't quite convince. More likely, the young Ewan McGregor had no grand masterplan beyond an abstract notion of movie stardom. He was just existing day to day, enjoying his youth, surviving school. Chances are that he knew he would leave Crieff one day, but for the time being he neither hated the place nor allowed himself to be entirely seduced by it. Catapults, fireworks and Presley impersonations aside, it was an unusually mature and philosophical approach for one so young.

However, in the spring of 1987, this sleepy apprenticeship was drawing to a close. Henceforth life would move a little quicker for Ewan McGregor. First port of call (one week after quitting school) was Perth Repertory Theatre. Upon leaving Morrison's, McGregor took a six-month unpaid placement there; painting scenery, hefting props and studying the ways of professional actors first hand. Meanwhile, he continued to live at home, shuttling the thirteen miles back-and-forth between Crieff and Perth in his bottle-green Volkswagen Beetle.

Perth was no Glasgow or London, yet it proved a bracing new environment for the acting hopeful. 'I started learning about people and the way they lived their lives,' he recalls.

> I immediately started working backstage in the theatre where I met gay people and people who were having affairs. I met poncy actors and good actors, and I also started learning about the world, seeing things I'd never come across before in my small, conservative town.

He figures low down on the programme for Perth Theatre's production of *A Passage to India* in October 1987, grouped under the heading of 'Servants and Others' ('just running around in a turban all blacked up'). McGregor was in his element. 'My life,' he says with a grin, 'went into widescreen.'

From these roadie-style beginnings, it was a short step to a more legitimate base. First came a one-year foundation course in drama at the Kirkcaldy College of Technology: a multi-disciplinary montage of set building, costume design, acting and stage managing. It was this move that marked McGregor's proper break from Crieff, leaving his parents' home in favour of permanent accommodation at the college's hall of residence. He went out with Hannah Titley, a trainee set designer. He also began to hone his acting abilities, injecting his style with a professionalism which had been largely absent during his time in Perth. From here, London beckoned. 'I mean, I'm fiercely Scottish, totally patriotic and I will always consider myself a Scot,' Ewan insists.

> But London is the place to be if you really want to give it a go as an actor, and I think a lot of people found it daunting. I kind of got the impression that a lot of Scottish actors were scared of London. So that was the big step for me, really. "Go South, young man."

At first McGregor had designs on the Royal Academy of Dramatic Arts, but RADA rejected him after a cursory interview. A decade on, the experience still rankles: 'It was smile, shake hands and get shown the door; pointless me even showing up.' Guildhall School of Music and Drama, on the edge of London's East End, was his second choice. Its three-year acting course is gruelling and competitive: only twenty-five students are accepted annually from around seven hundred initial applicants. On the face of it, McGregor – inexperienced, relatively unconnected and hailing from a minor technical college in Fife – didn't stand much of a chance. But he was accepted, despite playing 'a piece of elastic' in his final audition. He was to find such frivolity a rare indulgence at Guildhall. Upon leaving, McGregor remembered it as an arduous time. His raw talent and general lack of intellectualizing cut against the grain of Guildhall's more formal mode of teaching. He claimed it made him feel awkward and self-conscious as a performer. 'I have never', he explains, 'been a cerebral actor. It all reeks of bullshit to me.' Where Perth Rep and Kirkcaldy had been fun, varied and practical, Guildhall appeared structured and over-serious – Morrison's Academy in more glamorous garb. As Kenneth Rea, who taught McGregor in mime and traditional drama argued,

> By the nature of a challenging training, a lot of it will take away somebody's confidence. But we hope that it assembles the student again at the end, with more confidence and greater technique.

Their star pupil, with his long-standing dislike of formal education, remained sceptical.

As he had at Morrison's, McGregor endured his instruction. He was happier onstage than in class and on one occasion, pre-empting his later experiences on *Trainspotting*, McGregor performed a show at a drugs rehabilitation centre. He also made half-hearted attempts to realize his rock-star ambitions, penning maudlin three-chord love-letters to Scotland and supplementing his grant by busking at Bank tube station with an actor friend, Zubin Varla. On Sunday evenings he and Varla would play covers at a vegetarian restaurant in south London under the name Mano et Manot. His finest song, he would later claim, was entitled 'Pocketful of Ticket Stubs'. 'You don't need to worry babe,' went its angst-ridden refrain, 'I'm not in any pain/Just the thing that stops me going mad/Is me slowly going insane.' Fortunately, perhaps, such guitar-hero aspirations remained an artistic sideline. Acting was always Ewan McGregor's first and deepest love.

His big break came quickly. It instantly broke him out of the crowd of other student hopefuls and brought his projected three-year stint at Guildhall to a premature end. When he fled Morrison's Academy, McGregor had been taking a leap into the darkness. This time he had somewhere definite to go. In March 1992, following a successful audition for Dennis Potter and director Rennie Rye, he was contracted to play Mike Hopper, one of the two principal roles in Potter's *Lipstick on Your Collar*. 'It came out of nowhere,' recalls McGregor, 'and I couldn't fucking believe it.' In fact, the seeds of success had been sown a few months earlier, when a procession of agents and casting directors had attended Guildhall's students' open evening. McGregor had performed from a scene he had penned himself (a sketch about a Scottish oil rigger who'd lost his leg), had fluffed his lines and shuffled off feeling he'd bungled his chance. Agent Lindy King, seated in the audience, thought differently. After the show, she approached the aspiring actor. Ewan McGregor was on his way.

● ● ● ● ●

A lead role in a prime-time TV serial would prove a heady debut for any budding actor. A lead role in a Dennis Potter project is something else again. Not yet twenty-one, McGregor could not have wished for a better launchpad.

Born into a working-class family in the Forest of Dean, Potter had risen via Oxford and the BBC's training ground to become Britain's most well-known and respected TV dramatist. Where other writers traditionally aspired towards film screenplays or novels, Potter stuck predominantly to television. It was, he always claimed, the most purely democratic medium; one which was suited to the populist leanings of a man who in his youth had run for Parliament as a prospective Labour MP. Throughout his career Potter came in for criticism for his perceived misogyny and the general dark, acid tone of his writing. Yet few could deny that he had raised television drama to a new level, infusing an often lightweight art-form with the fire of his insight and originality. His *Blue Remembered Hills*, *Vote Vote Vote for Nigel Barton*, and the controversial *Brimstone and Treacle* stand today as controversial peaks in homegrown TV drama.

Lipstick on Your Collar was, arguably, not quite up to the standard of these past triumphs. It was a little overstretched, a shade uneven and a bit too reliant on coming-of-age clichés. But, for all that, this six-part Channel 4 series fitted in neatly with the Potter *oeuvre*. Eventually screened in early 1993, *Lipstick on Your Collar* marked the final instalment in an informal trilogy preceded by the markedly superior *Pennies from Heaven* (which was set in the 1930s) and his bril-liant *The Singing Detective* (which cut between present-day and the 1940s). Fifties' London was the setting for *Lipstick on Your Collar*, an uncharacteristically traditional rites-of-passage drama about two bored and frustrated National Service kids adrift in the oppressive War Office during the Suez Crisis. McGregor played Hopper, a strutting Londoner. The co-starring role went to Giles Thomas, who played Potter-surrogate Francis, a shy, spluttering, scholarly Welshman obsessed with Russian literature. Old-style conservatism clashes against burgeon-ing rock and roll culture, obliquely represented by Hopper and peroxide vamp Sylvia (Louise Germaine), who shares Francis's dreary room. The whole thing comprises a clear-eyed, relatively unsentimental hymn to a new breed of British youth. Francis and Hopper are, outwardly, poles apart; one a swottish, highly educated son of a rural working-class family, the other a robust, cocksure city kid. Both, though, find their hopes and aspirations straitjacketed by a class-bound, callous and outmoded institution. By the end, both characters break out to find happiness and, potentially, a better way forward. Both, Potter implies, are part of a new generation; a new direction for British culture.

Potter had planned on directing *Lipstick on Your Collar* himself but Channel 4 had other plans. Mindful of the disastrous reception to 1989's BBC drama *Blackeyes* (which Potter both scripted and directed), station executives called in experienced TV director Rennie Rye to helm the project and so rein in Potter's trademark indulgences. Initially incensed by the decision, Potter eventually came to like and respect Rye (whom he later insisted should direct his last two tele-plays). He also took to visiting the set regularly throughout its protracted six-month shoot and took a fatherly interest in his young charges. On one occa-sion, Potter and McGregor were discussing the actor's future in a graveyard when, in the midst of a pep talk, Potter (notorious for his ill health) retreated to throw up behind a gravestone. 'That was very weird,' recalls McGregor. 'Here was this great master, and me trying to make a good impression, and he kept fucking puking up. After that I wasn't so bothered about impressing him.'

By this point Potter had yet to be diagnosed as suffering from the cancer which would eventually kill him. He died in June 1994, leaving behind two hurriedly written but affecting screenplays in *Karaoke* (in which McGregor would cameo) and *Cold Lazarus*; an elegiac coda from one of drama's leading lights.

Like *Pennies from Heaven* and *The Singing Detective* before it, *Lipstick on Your Collar* took its life blood from the popular song, with extended, fantastical mime sequences woven throughout the otherwise naturalistic action. It was a technique Potter had made his own. 'Cheap songs, so called, actually do have something of the Psalms of David about them,' Potter remarked during his compulsive 1994 interview with Melvyn Bragg. 'They do say the world is other than it is. They do illuminate.' During the course of shooting, McGregor mimed his way through a whole host of early rock and roll standards, and did so with such panache that a record producer subsequently badgered him to cut an album of fifties covers. McGregor baulked at such cash-in tackiness: 'Luckily I said no straight away. I would have had the shortest career in history. I'd be in Robson and Jerome land now.' Learning to say no, and resisting grabbing at the first opportunities that present themselves, is a crucial lesson for every young actor. On this occasion, McGregor's natural instinct served him well.

McGregor remembers counting the days before *Lipstick on Your Collar* began screening. At the time, he was performing in Joe Orton's *What the Butler Saw* on stage at the Salisbury Playhouse. McGregor thought that *Lipstick* would bring him instant fame and act as his passport to stardom. But in the end, his role was inevitably less attention-grabbing than that of Giles Thomas (who played the more showy part). Even vampish Louise Germaine made an impact. Her pouting pose cropped up on advertising hoardings and apparently caused a road accident when one rubber-necking motorist ran into the back of another.

Yet in terms of work offers, Lipstick on Your Collar served its purpose. Although, immediately after shooting, McGregor fell into a brief spell of unemployment. 'I dealt with that very badly,' he confesses.

> It wasn't something I was used to and in hindsight it all feels a bit pathetic. I was raging about, full of self-pity, thinking I'd never work again. Totally self-indulgent, prima-donna behaviour. I needed someone just to slap me and tell me I was being a right little bastard.

Four months later the work started coming in, and the trickle became a flood. There was the Orton play in Salisbury, then advertising voice-overs (debuting with a St Ivel Gold commercial), and a starring role in an eleven-minute short, *Family Style*, for the inaugural year of Channel 4's Lloyd's Bank Film Challenge. *Family Style* was written by seventeen-year-old Matthew Cooper and found McGregor playing a young man coming to terms with the death of his brother. 'I fucking love that little film,' McGregor would say years later. 'I was so proud of that.'

This cluster of work culminated in a stint across the Channel playing in a BBC adaptation of Stendhal's nineteenth-century adventure *Scarlet and Black*. With his hair dyed black, McGregor took the role of Julien Sorel, seducing and swashbuckling a merry dash through period France. In terms of public profile, this glossy, populist swashbuckler made a great splash. In the week *Scarlet and Black* began screening, McGregor landed on the cover of the *Radio Times*, which hailed him as 'a mixture of passion and level-headedness, of innocence and sex-appeal'.

1993 also witnessed McGregor's first stab at a feature film. Fittingly, it was for Scottish director Bill Forsyth, who had risen to fame on the back of such soulful slice-of-life comedies as *That Sinking Feeling*, *Comfort and Joy* and, most notably, *Local Hero*. This 1983 hit told the beguiling tale of an American oil-company's proposed takeover of a remote fishing village and had starred, alongside Burt Lancaster and Peter Reigert, Ewan's uncle Denis Lawson as a libidinous hotel owner. Ten years on, though, Forsyth's career was in a perilous state. A clutch of American movies such as *Housekeeping* and *Breaking In* had met with little success and, in hindsight, *Being Human* only seems to have made matters worse.

Being Human was a typically Forsythian creature: quirky and eccentric. Its structure takes the form of a series of five time-travelling vignettes that charts the adventures of a bungling everyman figure (played by Robin Williams) from the Bronze Age to the present day. McGregor hung out in Morocco for a month and pops up in the movie's fourth segment, playing a Portuguese castaway called Alvarez. But his contribution is negligible. He has two lines ('I'll do it,' and 'It was a joke, it was a joke!') and then vanishes.

The film itself took much the same route. Following disastrous test previews in the United States, *Being Human* was hastily and heavily re-edited for a swift and painful run at the cinemas. New York style-Bible *Village Voice* praised its 'wonderful, subtle perversities', but the film proved to be a box-office bomb. In Britain, its fate was still more ignominious. Denied a theatrical release, *Being Human* bypassed the cinemas and travelled straight to video. According to Forsyth, his film was 'conceived and designed as an anarchist movie . . . I was,' he added, 'trying to write a poem.' But poems and anarchy invariably translate into box-office poison, and for all its manifest charm, this 'queer duck' of a movie (as critic Leonard Maltin called it) failed to find an audience. Disillusioned, Forsyth turned his back on film-making. He has not made another picture to date.

Being Human closed a chapter in McGregor's life too. His whistle-stop apprenticeship was drawing to a close. Behind him lay an inauspicious feature film, a popular BBC adventure yarn and a starring role in a work by Britain's leading dramatist. For an actor in his early twenties this was an enviable record. But the acting profession is built on notoriously shaky foundations. McGregor had bashed out a decent launchpad for himself, yet a few wrong moves and a bungled job or two would usher him right back into obscurity. What he needed now was a break-through movie; something which would inscribe him indelibly on to the public mind. The forecast, however, seemed unpromising. British cinema was languishing in the doldrums and choice roles for talented young actors looked as rare as hens' teeth. In 1993, the safest bet for a talented young actor seemed to be to stay put in television. Creatively it was less rewarding, but the work was more consistent.

● ● ● ● ●

Just before Christmas, Ewan McGregor showed up – fashionably late – at the star-spangled *Radio Times* covers party (an invitee thanks to featuring in the magazine's *Scarlet and Black* lead story). One fellow guest remembers him drunk as a lord, flanked by a doting hoard of hangers-on:

> Nobody seemed quite sure whether he was gay or not. It was that mad, end-of-party time and everyone was trying to pull everyone else. Ewan was the pick of the bunch and was just surrounded by lusty men and women, looking utterly bemused in the middle. I thought the whole thing was about to turn ugly.

'I love any kind of bash,' McGregor muses, 'and I'm always the last person to leave. I stay there right through to the fucking bitter end.' For Ewan McGregor, though, the real party had barely begun.

BRITISH CINEMA BURIED

2. BRITISH CINEMA BURIED

If not quite a desert, the British film scene in the early nineties was no place for a young-gun actor to earn his spurs. Production was down, and though cinema admissions were rising steadily out of their mid-eighties nadir, homegrown pictures were taking only the thinnest cut of the box-office returns. This was partly down to the vagaries of the UK distribution system: a territory dominated by big American companies with exclusive ties to the principal cinema chains. With the market carved up in their favour, Hollywood blockbusters inevitably took centre-stage. By contrast, the most realistic hope for a Brit-backed movie was a limited run on the art-house periphery. More often than not they were smothered at birth. Of the sixty-seven films produced during 1993, more than half remained unwanted and unreleased a year down the line. Meanwhile, Hollywood accounted for 95 per cent of the pictures on show at British cinemas.

There were, however, other factors at work. With hindsight, it's easy to view the early nineties as a time of near unprecedented creative turmoil; an era in uneasy transition. Within this subsistence industry three lines of thought dominated. The first (and most commercially viable) was the niche carved out by Ismail Merchant and James Ivory. Throughout a long, profitable collaboration,

Indian-born producer Merchant and American-born director Ivory became the auteurs of a form of plush period cinema, bolstered by intelligent scripts and predominantly stage-trained performers. At home their pictures drew uniformally decent reviews and did respectable box-office business. But Merchant–Ivory's genius was in accessing the US market; a crucial breakthrough if a British picture were to recoup its production costs. When they attempted American-set pictures (*Slaves of New York*, *Mr and Mrs Bridge*), the team came a-cropper. But Merchant–Ivory were in their element rustling up impeccably textured portraits of a bygone Britain, designed predominantly for foreign consumption. With such films as *A Room with A View*, *Howard's End* and *The Remains of the Day*, they became – incongruously, given their respective backgrounds – British cinema's most reliable export.

Not everyone was enamoured of the Merchant–Ivory approach. Director Alan Parker famously slated their output as 'Laura Ashley cinema': all pretty frocks, flowing locks and *Homes and Gardens* decor. Certainly there was something suspiciously deodorized about the Merchant–Ivory depiction of British culture. Its angst was forever pushed way below the surface and its drama sometimes seemed a mere accompaniment to the ambience. Period settings aside, this was a Britain unrecognizable to the vast majority of its inhabitants, a nostalgic never-never land strung somewhere between history and Hollywood.

In the second camp sat the old guard. Throughout the 1960s the homegrown industry had been given a shot in the arm by the Free Cinema/'kitchen sink' output of such directors as Tony Richardson (*The Loneliness of the Long Distance Runner*), Ken Loach (*Cathy Come Home*) and Lindsay Anderson (*If . . .*, *This Sporting Life*). Vigorously naturalistic in tone, these films blended social realism with the looser stylistic flurries of the French New Wave. When Tom

Courtenay's borstal boy thwarted the authorities by refusing to win his cross-country race and Richard Harris's blue-collar rugby hero spilled his aggression out at home, sides of British life rarely captured on celluloid were revealed. Quarter of a century on, this social-realist school – subtly modernized but essentially the same – still maintained a bolt-hole in the film landscape.

After a few rocky spells (when he earned his crust making TV commercials for Tetley's Bitter) Loach was making features again. In the meantime, Mike Leigh had graduated from teleplays with a series of acclaimed pictures which had the same aims and ideals as their 1960s precursors. Family sagas like *High Hopes* and *Life is Sweet* even found an audience in America and, particularly, in France, where Leigh was hailed as the ultimate chronicler of everyday British life. 'They treat me like a footballer over there,' Leigh once remarked.

These two modes of film-making were poles apart. The first was a shrewd repackage of one earlier age, the second increasingly seen as a stylistic hangover from another. Inevitably there had to be a third, more forward-thinking way.

The young tyro directors coming up in the nineties felt little affinity with either the Merchant–Ivory or the social-realist approach. Nor, it must be said, did they have much time for the country's more iconoclastic art-house outsiders (Peter Greenaway, Terence Davies, Derek Jarman). Instead they strove towards a more commercially driven, nakedly populist breed of film-making. Twentysomething movie-makers like Paul Anderson, Vadim Jean, Gary Sinyor and Danny Cannon tailored their natural enthusiasm for cinema with a post-Thatcherite, market-forces sensibility. 'Entertainment not art' was their rallying cry; modern-day Hollywood their obvious inspiration. 'My favourite films are made in Hollywood,' argued Vadim Jean.

> The mistake most British directors make is to make the same film again and again. Because they only have one idea or one thing to say. Me, I have nothing to say. Absolutely nothing to say. I have a very simplistic aim. I want to entertain people. What we've forgotten in the UK is that entertainment is the primary function of cinema. We don't make films for the 15–25 age group at the UCI Multiplex in Slough. I want to make those films. They are the bulk of the cinema-going audience.

His one-time partner Gary Sinyor agreed: 'If only the British would stop making art films. They seem to think commercial movies are bad.' It was into this third camp that Ewan McGregor would eventually fall.

The new style of Brit-pic didn't quite spring out of nowhere. If it had a precedent it came through the Palace Pictures stable of Stephen Woolley, Nik Powell and writer–director Neil Jordan, which flourished for a brief spell in the mid-1980s. Woolley's aim in producing Jordan's lush, fantastical *The Company of Wolves* had been to come up with a purely British film that could open at the Odeon, Leicester Square (the ultimate in populist big-screen venues). But Palace's Utopian ideals foundered as a result of commercially risky projects which brought fitful box-office returns. Following the disastrous reception to Julien Temple's costly 1986 pop-opera *Absolute Beginners* received in 1986, Palace found itself in a perpetual struggle to stay afloat. The company finally folded in 1992, just before Jordan's jolting IRA thriller *The Crying Game* (a huge Stateside hit) might have saved it. The new gang of rising film-makers sought to resurrect its ethos, albeit in a leaner, more commercially astute guise.

The first problem was finding the cash to make these pictures. Fortunately the climate was slowly changing. In the 1980s, Film on Four (the cinema wing of Channel 4 Television) had served as the muscle behind such projects as *My Beautiful Laundrette, Wish You Were Here* and Terence Davies's *Distant Voices, Still Lives* – all critically acclaimed British movies which enjoyed limited box-office returns. But in October 1990 David Aukin, the executive director of the Royal National Theatre, was brought in as the division's head, with an unofficial brief to hunt out more commercially viable scripts (although Aukin himself has always denied this was a specific instruction). At the time, this seemed a minor development, yet it would swell in significance as the years progressed. Eight years on, Channel 4 Films looks like being the lynchpin on which the current industry is based.

In the meantime, securing a solid budgetary commitment seemed virtually impossible, particularly if the prospective film-makers had no previous track record. For a short spell the grass-roots, DIY option suggested a possible way forward. Take the tactic adopted by unproven Vadim Jean and Gary Sinyor when making *Leon the Pig Farmer*, a spry comedy about a north London Jewish boy (Mark Frankel) who discovers he was born into Yorkshire farming stock. One of only twelve pure-bred British films produced in 1991, its pedigree was hugely idiosyncratic. Jean and Sinyor formed 'Leon the Pig Farmer plc' and raised a shoestring production pool of £155,000 through a share issue which pulled in private investors. The rest of the budget was funded on the basis of a deferred-payment scheme. Cast and crew agreed to work for nothing on the understanding that they would be paid if and when the film went into profit. 'Once you knock off the cast and crew salaries and persuade people to give equipment and facilities for free,' noted Sinyor wryly, 'you find out what you *really* have to spend.'

As an example of can-do initiative, of outsiders breaking through into a closed-shop system, *Leon the Pig Farmer* was a triumph. It was also a gamble on an epic scale: Sinyor likened it to 'climbing Everest stark naked', while Jean admitted that 'this is a desperate measure. It's not the way it should be.' The makers risked everything on their film finding an audience, and yet in the end (and despite sunny reviews) *Leon the Pig Farmer* found itself struggling, a victim of both the Hollywood domination of British cinema chains and audience reluctance to check out a small-scale curio without a big-name cast. Six years after *Leon the Pig Farmer*'s release, varous debts remain outstanding, with its creators remaining financially down on the deal.

Even as a calling-card, the film had limited impact. Sinyor laboured for several years to raise finance for his next project (the bungled romantic-comedy *Solitaire for Two*), and when eventually completed, the film disappeared from cinema screens within a matter of weeks. Jean fared only slightly better with his own solo projects, *Beyond Bedlam* and *Clockwork Mice* (which apparently played to just four ticket-buyers over the course of one weekend at a provincial cinema). In the case of Jean and Sinyor, breaking into the industry was just the opening hurdle. Maintaining momentum posed a whole new set of problems.

Beyond Bedlam, though, remains crucial in tracing the growth of a new kind of homegrown film. Made for £3 million and starring Keith Allen, Craig Fairbrass and Elizabeth Hurley, it's a picture in line with Jean's determination to forge an 'entertaining' brand of popular cinema. It is a beer-and-pizzas serial-killer yarn played out in a shadowy, labyrinthine lunatic asylum. Sheila Johnston, film critic on the *Independent*, was not impressed. 'I have seen the future of British cinema,' she wrote, 'and it looks dim.'

Here, in essence, was the manifesto of the new wave of young directors at work in the early nineties: a core of hard, fast pictures of mass-market appeal with straightforward (or 'high concept') scripts and plenty of action. Hip, vital and youth-targeted, these films tempted criticism in the way they nominated style over substance but at least this was a firm step away from the limitations of social realism.

This was the prevailing ethos, the 'third way forward' for British film production. In time, this formula would be honed and directed. Right now it was raw and over-eager: a tactic without a track record or a coherent infrastructure, and with only the vague, sniffing-the-wind sense that there was an audience out there. In retrospect, the first films of the Brit-brat vanguard seem like kamikaze bombers, breaking from their cover and burning up in an unfamiliar and unaccommodating climate. At the vanguard of this new frontier were directors Paul Anderson, Danny Cannon and Vadim Jean. More friends than rivals, they were all working towards the same end, visiting each other's shoots and discussing possible ways to break the industry deadlock.

First off the blocks was Danny Cannon, a graduate of the National Film and Television School in Beaconsfield, whose father had worked in film production. Aged twenty-five, the precocious Cannon made his debut in the summer of 1993 with *The Young Americans*, a fast-paced London-set detective thriller. *The Young Americans* boasted a voguish contemporary pop score (featuring Björk and the Stereo MCs), and had one eye fixed firmly on the US market (Harvey Keitel headlined as a fish-out-of-water American cop). Cannon made it 'to show the British film industry that you could make a good-looking, well-made, commercial movie for the same money that it costs to make an ambiguous, pretentious, dull movie. People either like it or they don't, but they can't say it's crap.'

Unfortunately for Cannon, they could. *The Young Americans* was put together with an obvious visual panache and boasted a clutch of neat action set pieces but, on the whole, was a soulless and tawdry affair. In tilting at a crossover market, Cannon bleached out all the nuances of its London backdrop in favour of a brash uniformity which could translate anywhere in the world with the minimum of culture shock. 'Everything about the film seems packaged, from the title down,' wrote critic Adam Mars Jones. 'Why the film is called *The Young Americans* remains a mystery,' mused the *Guardian*'s Derek Malcolm. 'Presumably because, if it had been called *The Young British* no one would go to see it.' As a battle-cry for a new British cinema, *The Young Americans* sounded a flat and feeble note.

Next up came Paul Anderson, who was twenty-seven at the time of shooting his debut picture, *Shopping*. Here was a film with a buzz about it. *Shopping* was a stylized, wilfully amoral overview of the ram-raid culture rife in Britain's inner cities. 'The growth crime in Europe and America at the moment is car crime,' reasoned Anderson. 'The car is *the* Western consumer object, that's why cars are so important to the kids who steal them. It's capitalism gone mad, a backlash against the "me generation" of the 1980s. The whole ethic of the eighties was that you had to get on your bike, you had to go out and take. We sowed the seeds ten years ago and now we're reaping the whirlwind.'

Newcastle-born Anderson had studied film theory at Warwick University. Behind the camera, he aspired towards the balletic visual sweep of French director Luc Besson (who was responsible for the cult hits *Subway* and *Nikita*). Together with producer Jeremy Bolt, Anderson assembled a montage of true-life ram-raid footage (culled from a police surveillance source) to raise cash for the project. David Aukin dubbed the tape 'a knock-out' and immediately put the film into development (its £2.5 million budget was eventually pieced together by Channel 4, PolyGram, German firm WMG and Japanese backers Kuzui Enterprises). Later, Bolt went to the Milan Film Festival touting around a goodie-bag of potential marketing tie-ins. '*Shopping*', explained Bolt, 'is about fashion, gadgets, music.' He proposed a line of commemorative key-rings, posters and specially designed bags with the 'S' in *Shopping* replaced by a dollar sign. Even from its conception, *Shopping* sounded an aggressively American attitude. Anderson and Bolt even toyed with the idea of putting an American actor in the lead but finally settled on twenty-year-old Londoner Jude Law to play the part of Billy, the film's joyriding anti-hero.

Shopping was shot during the summer of 1993 in the badlands around Canary Wharf. Its plot was speedy, straightforward and economical in every sense of the word. Teen-dream Billy, fresh out of jail, hooks up with feisty femme Jo (Sadie Frost) and cuts a car-jacking dash through some nameless nocturnal metropolis. Together, the pair of 'twoccers' (taken without owner's consent) pinch a red BMW and plan a daring 'cash and carry' raid on the glistening Retail Land shopping mall. But trouble, in the form of sneering rival Tommy (Sean Pertwee), is close behind. Cue explosive finale.

On the face of it, *Shopping* was a shrewd venture. Its ram-raid content guaranteed controversy and press coverage (the British Board of Film Censors sat nervously on the film for seven weeks before release). Anderson himself did little to dampen the controversy; hinting that he may have had first-hand knowledge of the craze from his own days knocking about in Newcastle's 'bandit country' and remarking that he was 'not so far removed from the generation of kids who are out there doing it'. Moreover *Shopping* boasted a pretty, trendy cast which, combined with artistic reconstructions of inner-city milieux, was a rare phenom-enon in modern British cinema. 'I go and look at these derelict, bleak urban landscapes,' said Andserson, 'and they're beautiful.' All told, *Shopping* looked to be shaping up for a well-judged beach-head targeted at that elusive 15–25 age group. 'Its not just Sega or Nintendo that's keeping kids away,' Bolt argued.

'They just don't get movies which are actually about them.' Meanwhile, Anderson's own theory echoed Woolley's decade-old wish for Palace Pictures' *The Company of Wolves*. 'My aim has always been to make a movie that would kick some ass in this country,' Anderson said, 'the kind of movie you could open in Leicester Square rather than a couple of art-house cinemas. But also a movie that could play abroad as well.'

The advance word was promising. The *Face* magazine dubbed it 'the sexiest British movie of the year' and reckoned it to be 'in your face and through the windscreen'. In the months leading up to its release in 1994, the *Shopping* bandwagon looked to be rolling along nicely. Cosy British cinema was about to be shaken to the core.

Except, of course, that it didn't turn out quite like that. Like Cannon's *The Young Americans*, *Shopping* lacked heart and weight and any real conviction beyond a desperate grope towards some abstract concept of cool. Although its producer and director were both in their twenties, it had the look and feel of a cold corporate venture assembled by middle-aged businessmen. Its sloganeering 'yoof-speak' fell embarrassingly flat. Its screeching, soundtrack-driven action looked calculatedly tailored for the most gnat-like of attention spans. Plus, in stylizing their subject out of all existence, *Shopping* left itself in a kind of limbo. It was neither true enough in its depiction to resonate with its target audience, nor accessible enough for mainstream audiences. Buoyed up higher than it deserved on a wave of hype, *Shopping* came back down to earth with a bang. Though the film eventually went into profit, the box-office performance was essentially lacklustre.

Shopping, *Beyond Bedlam* and *The Young Americans* all promised an energetic alternative to the stuffy traditions of homegrown film production. So, too, did *White Angel*, a stiff, static serial-killer romp which its makers presumably hoped would cash-in on the Frederick and Rosemary West scandal that was dominating the headlines in the weeks running up to its release. Yet all these forays failed, and did so conspicuously. The new dream of British movie-making looked to have foundered before it had scarcely begun.

Ironically, perhaps, there was one genuinely edgy, youthful, vibrant and defiantly British picture during those dog-days of 1993–4. Unfortunately for the Cannon gang, it came courtesy of die-hard, old-school Mike Leigh.

In many respects this was an unnerving development, since Leigh was traditionally perceived as hailing from the old guard of directors. He had satirized middle-class aspiration in *Abigail's Party*, probed inner-city lifestyles in *Mean Time* and family strife in *High Hopes* and 1991's breakthrough film, *Life is Sweet*. His pictures were script-based; evolving out of long, painstaking improvised rehearsal schedules with the actors. In contrast to the pop-promo dynamism of Anderson and Cannon, Leigh didn't do much with the camera. In terms of visual style, his work was still, unflashy: a simple tool to frame the action. He was a director, not a distractor and, needless to say, his films never opened at the Odeon, Leicester Square. He was, in short, the epitome of everything that the *Shopping* brigade was fighting against.

But 1993's *Naked* threw Mike Leigh abruptly into a new direction. His set-up and mode of operation were the same, yet, in terms of tone and content, the film spectacularly broke away from the director's previous world-in-miniature approach. 'Having done the likes of *High Hopes* and *Life is Sweet*,' said Leigh, 'I felt it was time to do something that put the boot in a bit more.'

Naked tells the tale of Johnny (David Thewlis); twenty-seven, unemployed and over-stimulated. Turning up in London from his native Manchester, he crashes for a night with ex-girlfriend Louise (Lesley Sharp), beds her fragile goth flatmate, Sophie (Katrin Cartlidge), then embarks on a hellish odyssey through the city. On his travels he hooks up with two Glaswegian derelicts (future *Trainspotting* stars Ewen Bremner and Susan Vidler) and a lonesome night-watchman (Peter Wright). *Naked* offers little hope for its driven protagonist. The last shot has Johnny limping dementedly down the street, shambling off towards an uncertain future which one can only assume is bleak.

Deep down, *Naked* wasn't fundamentally different from Leigh's other work. It was, in essence, a social-realist drama; an impassioned assault on Thatcher's legacy and what Leigh regarded as the Major government's mis-management of Britain (one iconic shot has Johnny slumped beneath a protest poster reading 'Sack Major Not The Miners'). Thewlis's character emerges as the poisoned product of a bad society. He is bright, witty, occasionally charming, but paralysed by frustration. His energies have turned inward and backfired. But Leigh's dystopic vision extends further than this. For paralleling Johnny's story goes that of sociopathic yuppie Jeremy (Greg Crutwell). In society's terms, Johnny is a failure and Jeremy a success, but Leigh reveals them both to be hope-lessly damaged; the first's anguished self-loathing balanced by the other's icy, fascistic cruelty. Both, Leigh seems to be saying, are victims of a country descend-ing to hell in a hand-cart.

Stylistically, though, *Naked* hardly broke from the past. One critic viewed it as Leigh's version of *O Lucky Man* (Lindsay Anderson's classic picaresque film from the seventies). Another called its anguished main character 'a Jimmy Porter for the nineties'. It was also likened to an update of John Osborne's classic anti-hero drama, *Look Back in Anger*. *Naked* did not boast guns or car chases, balletic violence or dreamily lit visuals. Its characters were, by and large, ground-down, everyday folk with clothes and posture a million miles away from an *iD* fashion spread.

At heart, then, *Naked* was just reinvigorated kitchen sink. But what a transformation. Leigh's film was energetic, impactful and beautifully savage. Detractors complained about what they saw as the director's latent misogyny surging spectacularly to the fore. Undeniably, the picture made for uncomfortable viewing, but it was brilliant nonetheless: a sustained howl of rage set to celluloid.

Much of *Naked*'s success can be attributed to David Thewlis, who lent the character of Johnny a manic, mordant wit. Working in tamden with Leigh, the Blackpool-born actor evolved the character through recollections of people he had known. He hung out with Hare Krishnas, crammed up on Chaos Theory and injected Johnny's dialogue with a garbled kind of genius. 'They say it's a jungle out there,' he sneers on being led through an office block infested with foliage, 'they should see it in here.' It was in this scene, too, that Thewlis was allowed to cut loose. His giddying rant before Peter Wright's bemused nightwatchman took in Nostradamus, the Bible, Nazism and supermarket bar codes and somehow made them gel together. This was a *tour de force* set-piece, made all the more astounding by virtue of Leigh shooting the whole scene in a single take.

Thewlis deservedly scooped the Best Actor award at Cannes, but living inside Johnny's skin had taken its toll. 'My health suffered,' he said. 'I was smoking a lot and drinking a lot of coffee.' Following the film's wrap, he suffered a minor collapse; an understandable result of his Method approach, putting his psyche through the wringer to squeeze out the best possible performance. 'I wouldn't like to make out that acting in *Naked* almost killed me,' he reflected. 'But it didn't do me much good, that's for sure.'

For a short spell following *Naked*'s release it looked as though Thewlis was destined to move on to bigger, better things. He was young, British, vastly talented and had found, through Leigh, the perfect, emblematic showcase. If directors were casting their nets for the symbol of a new generation of home-grown players, Thewlis looked the obvious bet. But this was not to be. In the years since *Naked*, Thewlis has embarked on an eccentric clutch of career choices. He cropped up in one kids' movie (*Black Beauty*) and then worked on another (*James and the Giant Peach*). He was lured to Hollywood to work with Marlon Brando (on John Frankenheimer's schlocky *The Island of Dr Moreau*), then played second fiddle to Brad Pitt on the flat Himalayan epic *Seven Years in Tibet*. Of his post-Leigh *oeuvre*, only a vibrant, shaven-headed cameo in the Coen brothers' *The Big Lebowski* crackled with the energy of old. In terms of iconic status, Thewlis's chance had come and gone in the blink of an eye.

Even so, *Naked* remains a powerful achievement for all involved. In the doldrums of the early nineties cinema scene, it glittered balefully like a flinty diamond. You might love it, you might hate it, but either way, it was a hard film to ignore. Mike Leigh's old-bones-in-new-clothing approach had a cultural impact the Brit-brat directors could only dream of. Compared with *Naked*, *Shopping*, *The Young Americans* and *Beyond Bedlam* looked paltry fare indeed.

So what went wrong with the front line of Brit-brat cinema? In theory their ideals seemed sound: sharp, mid-budget, genre-led pictures that placed entertainment over art; brash youthfulness over staid middle age. And yet if the aim was to regenerate British cinema, the whole project came to nought.

With hindsight, one could argue that the seeds of destruction were right there at the point of conception. *Shopping*, *The Young Americans* and *Beyond Bedlam* were determinedly American in flavour. They strove to duplicate the

Hollywood formula and then transplant it wholesale to a different backdrop. If British kids want Hollywood movies, they argued, we'll give them Hollywood movies – but with British accents. Except that the transplant didn't work. As David Aukin explained:

> The British films that work in the marketplace are those which are different and have an integrity about them. If you just try to ape Hollywood, you're on a loser, because Hollywood does it better.

Director Hugh Hudson (who had triggered a minor renaissance twelve years earlier with *Chariots of Fire*) was still more gloomy: 'There's nothing original in British cinema today. It's the bastardization of any other cinema you like to name. Instead of speaking English, it speaks American.'

It is an old but apt truism: in order to be international you must first be national. Anderson and Cannon found themselves in a no-man's land, caught somewhere between wanting to make Hollywood-style blockbusters, and trying to present a gritty version of British youth culture. In the event, they failed on both counts. *Shopping* and *The Young Americans* were too 'British' to find a toe-hold in the mainstream US market, yet felt too 'phoney' and low budget to scoop up the youth market at home. Merchant–Ivory's tourist-book view of moneyed, middle-class Britain continued to be the best tactic for a commercial crossover. In 1994 writer Richard Curtis, producer Duncan Kenworthy and direc-tor Mike Newell suggested another way. Their romantic-comedy, *Four Weddings and a Funeral*, presented an idealized view of present-day England. It inserted an American star (Andie Macdowell) as the love interest and – hey presto – became the most commercially successful British picture ever made, with the bulk of its receipts coming from an intoxicated American public. It also made an overnight star of winsome Englishman Hugh Grant (who had previously made his name in Merchant–Ivory's *Maurice*).

The *Four Weddings* success was heartening, but its underlying message gave cause for concern. Curtis and Newell's jackpot formula struck many observers as reductive. The world of *Four Weddings and a Funeral* was merely a theme-park Britain: a landscape of sunny flats, sporty cars and endless soirées peopled by wealthy, witty characters untroubled by inconveniences such as holding down a job. Like Merchant–Ivory, it peddled a vision of England that was romantic but false. In terms of a healthy, self-sustaining British film industry, this was not the route to go down.

The Brit-brats offered an alternative but the mix wasn't right. In fact, Cannon and Anderson had more in common with the Merchant–Ivory school than they might like to admit. Their films nominally hoisted the cultural flag but were otherwise fixated on America. More than that, one got the impression that, rather than starting an artistic renaissance, their main aim was to flee Britain for a job in the States. *Shopping* and *The Young Americans* looked more like directorial calling-cards than organic, authentic movies. In this respect they succeeded admirably. After *The Young Americans*, Cannon was snapped up by Hollywood to helm a big-budget treatment of the *Judge Dread* comic-strip, with Sylvester Stallone in the title role. He has not made another film in the UK since. Likewise, Anderson also headed west to make *Mortal Kombat*, a misconceived film treatment of the ultra-violent computer game, which was followed up with the big-budget sci-fi horror *Event Horizon*.

Perhaps this was always their intention; perhaps a result of the problems of producing successful films at home. The migration of home-grown talent to the States has been a feature of the industry since Hitchcock. This time it sent a bad message. An attempt had been made to re-energize British film-making and it had failed. Its pioneers had simply packed up and moved on.

The formula undoubtedly needed reappraisal. It called for an overhaul and some tuning-up. Most importantly, it needed stories that came from the fabric of the culture and would resonate with the public. It had to be inherently British before it could be anything else.

In 1993 Ewan McGregor turned twenty-two. He was still learning his craft, earning his spurs. He had acted in *Lipstick on Your Collar* and *Scarlet and Black*, and made an inauspicious feature debut in *Being Human*, yet he was still very much an industry outsider looking in. So, to a lesser extent, was Danny Boyle, a thirty-seven-year-old director with a good track-record in television but still without a feature film to his name. So, too, was twenty-seven-year-old Andrew Macdonald, a wannabe producer on the fringes of the business, and twenty-nine-year-old John Hodge, an Edinburgh-based doctor with a yen to write screenplays. Together, these four were about to revitalize an industry in crisis spectacularly. Out of the ashes of the Brit-brats' failure would come a new way forward.

Shallow Grave began shooting in September.

OUT OF THE GRAVEYARD

3. OUT OF THE GRAVEYARD

This is how the jigsaw fits together. In August 1991 Andrew Macdonald ran into John Hodge amid the chaotic ebb and flow of the Edinburgh Film Festival. Hodge, a Glaswegian, was at the time serving as a junior doctor at the Edinburgh Royal Infirmary; getting up at the crack of dawn to put in a few hours' writing before his working day began. Macdonald, meantime, was working as a location manager on *Taggart*, the Scottish police detective TV series (though he also had a short film, *Dr Reitzer's Fragment*, playing at the festival).

In fact, this history-making encounter had been on the cards for months. Hodge's sister, Grace, had worked as an editor on Macdonald's short, and had mentioned that her brother was a budding screenwriter. When the pair eventually met, Hodge handed over a handwritten draft of the script that was to become *Shallow Grave*. Together the pair began developing it into something that might just work, with Macdonald picking it apart and Hodge piecing it back together again.

The process was made easier since Hodge and Macdonald shared a similar outlook. Both were disillusioned with the current crop of British movies and aspired towards a leaner, cleaner, more populist brand of cinema. 'We felt that a lot of film-making in Britain was totally lacking in ambition,' recalls Hodge, 'and we were never interested in making a well-regarded art-film.' For Macdonald's part, 'the films I like are not difficult-to-understand European art movies. But I equally find painful stuff like *Twister* and *Jurassic Park II*.'

As with Anderson, Cannon and Jean, modern American cinema was again the inspiration. This time, though, it came with a crucial difference. Rather than attempting to ape the big Hollywood entertainments, Macdonald and Hodge aspired towards the more taut, intelligent work of the US indie scene, which in the early nineties was being galvanized by the likes of Hal Hartley, John Dahl and the Coen brothers. In 1992, the approach became crystallized still more. Quentin Tarantino, a former video-store clerk in Los Angeles, employed a limited budget and minimal locations to craft a taut heist thriller in his debut feature, *Reservoir Dogs*. *Shallow Grave*'s duo were highly impressed. Explained Hodge:

> I'd seen a succession of American films which had one thing in common – a small group of people working out their differences in a tight situation over a short period of time. With the script for *Shallow Grave* it was important that something happened every page or so. The story moves so quickly that there's no time for the characters to spend heart-searching over the rights and wrongs of their actions.

Fittingly, *Shallow Grave* was initially conceived as an America-set thriller, with Bill Murray, Bridget Fonda and *GoodFellas* star Ray Liotta as Macdonald's dream-team cast, to play the three back-stabbing flatmates (Uma Thurman, Johnny Depp, John Cusack and Patricia Arquette were also mooted as possible alternatives). But Hodge and Macdonald were both Scots, and north of the border was the setting they felt most familiar with. From early on in their conversations, it became clear that a low-budget British thriller was the best route for *Shallow Grave*. It was to be a long, tough haul.

For Hodge, *Shallow Grave* was a sideline project that bloomed fantastically to become a way of life. For Macdonald it was his big chance; his belated break into mainstream film production. Still only in his mid-twenties, Macdonald had nonetheless already served a healthy apprenticeship in the engine-rooms of the film industry. Having quit school at eighteen, he worked unpaid at the newly opened National Film and Television School in Beaconsfield before blagging a job as a production-runner on Hugh Hudson's ill-fated *Revolution* (alongside *Absolute Beginners*, this was one of the big-budget disasters that so devastated the eighties film scene). From this wreckage he hopped across to the States, script-reading for Ocean Pictures and assisting director Zelda Barron on the Bridget Fonda teen caper *Shag*. Back in England, Macdonald served as assistant director on *Venus Peter*, then worked the locations on the Liam Neeson star vehicle *The Big Man* and Terence Davies's languid autobiography *The Long Day Closes*. As a training ground, Macdonald's apprenticeship ran a broad gamut. It took in all aspects of the home-grown film spectrum: wasteful, big-budget flops, low-key curios, brave failures and fringey, art-house efforts. He felt he knew precisely what didn't work; now he wanted to find out what did.

To fulfil this ambition, Macdonald cast further back for a reference point. His grandfather was the late Hungarian-born screenwriter, Emeric Pressburger. Alongside director Michael Powell, Pressburger had been responsible for some of the finest pictures of the 1940s. Outwardly different (Emeric was solid and quiet; Michael extrovert and extravagant), Powell and Pressburger worked in neat symbiosis. As 'the Archers', they took joint credit for their films, [all 'written, produced and directed by Michael Powell and Emeric Pressburger'] and came up with a clutch of beautifully idiosyncratic, perfectly accessible and purely British movies (*The Life and Death of Colonel Blimp, A Canterbury Tale, A Matter of Life and Death, The Red Shoes*). Macdonald felt that the Powell–Pressburger approach suggested a possible way forward: teamwork as opposed to individual vision; collaboration as opposed to movie-biz megalomania. Or, as director Danny Boyle would later put it: 'I don't think we produce great auteurs in this country. I don't think it's part of our culture. The really great work comes from partnerships.'

Within three years, the triumvirate of Boyle, Macdonald and Hodge, with Ewan McGregor as their chosen muse, would become a film-making partnership to rival the best.

In the meantime, there was money to raise. Legend has it that the man truly responsible for kickstarting *Shallow Grave* was David Aukin's chauffeur. In November 1992, the Channel 4 Films kingpin was in Inverness attending its annual Movie-Makers Session when Macdonald badgered his driver to pass on a copy of the script. Aukin read it, liked what he saw and set up a meeting with Hodge and Macdonald at Channel 4's London offices just before Christmas. By the following summer the budget was finally in place. *Shallow Grave* was generated by a commitment of £150,000 by the Glasgow Film Fund, with the rest coming from Channel 4. The final budget was £1,043,000.

Danny Boyle was the first new recruit to be 'auditioned' by Macdonald and Hodge. 'Andrew was looking for someone who was willing to work collaboratively,' recalls the director. 'He didn't want someone with a huge track record, like a Stephen Frears or a Terry Gilliam who was going to take over the script.' Macdonald agrees:

> The sort of person we needed was someone who was about to make their name. We didn't want an established name or someone who had tried and failed. We wanted someone who was our equivalent, but a more experienced film-maker.

Boyle fitted the bill. A native of Manchester – working class and grammar-school educated – he had developed a taste for cinema through watching European New Wave flicks at his local flea-pit. 'I used to go there to see sex,' he admits. 'But I came home having seen these incredible films – Bertolucci, Truffaut, Chabrol – and that was what I really fed on.' His first creative work was in theatre, where he rose to become deputy director of the Royal Court. But he found stage work to be 'an actor's tool'. Cinema, he felt, was the real way forward and a stint at BBC Belfast subsequently led him into film-making. Before *Shallow Grave*, he had helmed several episodes of *Inspector Morse* and the plush BBC mini-series *Mr Wroe's Virgins*. At the time of first meeting Macdonald and Hodge, Boyle was itching to have a go at a feature film. When he compared the script to the Coen brothers' *Blood Simple*, Macdonald knew they had their man. 'In conversation he came across as a man of sensitivity and endless patience but with a thuggish streak and a sort of low, animal cunning,' Hodge notes ruefully in his introduction to the *Shallow Grave* screenplay; 'in short, a man who could work with actors.'

Next came the players. First on board was Kiwi actress Kerry Fox, the most experienced of the acting trio. She had starred as turbulent writer Janet Frame in Jane Campion's stately *An Angel at my Table*, and worked alongside Boyle on *Mr Wroe's Virgins*. She was contracted to play Juliet, the cool medic who becomes the film's most complex and unpredictable character. At first Fox was reluctant. The *Shallow Grave* script read as cold and cruel to her: 'A bunch of nasty people fighting with each other over money,' she recalls. 'I didn't think it was up my street.' She was swayed by her healthy earlier collaboration with Boyle and by a few meetings with Macdonald. 'Andrew was the factor really,' she recalls. 'It was so amazing having a producer who was of a similar age. It made the whole thing feel so much more natural and collaborative, as though we were all part of a big team.'

Fox's role was a tricky and layered affair, and one which necessitated a good deal of homework. To get fully into character, Fox studied the films of Kim Novak to perfect just the right strain of chill carnality; then scrutinized the paintings of Paula Rego, whose fairytale imagery boasts a similarly strange strain of off-beat sensuality. 'On the surface Juliet doesn't give much away, keeps her cards very close to her chest,' reckons Fox, 'but underneath there's a lot of tumult going on. She's a very strange person, and an awkward person to make out, even for me.'

The peach part, though, was that of David, the quiet accountant who slides into spooky psychosis. This role fell to twenty-nine-year-old Christopher Eccleston, a rising star who was playing opposite Robbie Coltrane in TV's *Cracker* at the time. Eccleston looked back on his previous work with a faint contempt. A year earlier, the Manchester-born actor had co-starred in Alex Cox's *Death and the Compass* – a wilfully convoluted adaptation of an existential Borges short story, which was well received by practically everyone except the actor himself (he remarked that 'it didn't really mean anything to me'). Before that, he had debuted in *Let Him Have It*, a flat account of the infamous Craig Bentley murder case from the 1950s. Eccleston starred as Bentley yet had loathed the finished product: 'It was sentimental, it was woolly liberal armchair bollocks, and I was crap in it.'

Shallow Grave, then, was to offer a new beginning for Christopher Eccleston; the role of David Stephens a fresh challenge for this most serious-minded of actors. While admitting that the character is 'a bit of a Terry Pratchett reader', he says, 'I wanted to avoid doing the Monty Python chartered accountant.' In Eccleston's hands, a stock cultural cliché was to become something loopy, strange and worryingly unpredictable.

Ewan McGregor was to fit the third vacancy. Alex Law is the cocky young newshound who emerges as the tale's most openly dynamic character; a young hot-shot who becomes a vegetarian because it offers 'an interesting counterpoint to his otherwise callous personality'. At the time of casting, McGregor was cropping up each Sunday night in Dennis Potter's *Lipstick on Your Collar*, and his edgy vitality was just what the film-makers were looking for. By all accounts, he instantly gelled with both Boyle and Macdonald (having written the script, Hodge had by this time faded into the background somewhat). 'Right from the start he was a bit of a dream come true,' says Boyle. 'You get them every so often – thoroughbreds. Whatever you ask them to do they give it straight back to you, absolutely accurately. It does exhaust you a bit as a director.'

McGregor, for his part, took to the role of Alex with gusto: 'The only time you see him speaking to people he's being rude . . . The whole thing hinges on his yearning for Juliet. He wants her so badly – and that's quite a nice quality in him – that you like him and begin to see him as a bit of a loveable bastard.' In preparation for his role, McGregor hung out at the newsroom of the *Evening Times* in Glasgow, to find an angle for Alex's journalistic background. On a more esoteric level, he also listened to tapes of various stand-ups: Billy Connolly, Dennis Leary (a personal favourite of his) and off-beat American duo the Jerky Boys, in order to catch Alex's biting intonation and cruel knack with a put-down. After *Scarlet and Black* and *Lipstick on Your Collar*, this was to be Ewan's debut role on Scottish soil. 'It's the first thing I've ever done in contemporary clothing,' he remarked at the time, 'which is much harder, because I've got nothing to hide behind – no cravats, no English accent.'

Shallow Grave is a modern-day *film noir*; a B-movie in contemporary duds; a Scottish variant on the American indie gems of John Dahl and the Coen brothers. Boyle, though, also claimed the thrillers of Alfred Hitchcock and Billy Wilder as equal inspirations. 'I suppose the film is cruel,' he was to say. 'But then life can be cruel and cold. There are other sides of life, of culture, but *Shallow Grave* doesn't choose to look at them.'

Few debuts open so compellingly as *Shallow Grave*. Leftfield's thrumming dance track ushers the viewer on a breakneck tour of Edinburgh, while Chris Eccleston's voice-over intones flatly in the background (the tactic was so successful that the team would repeat it on *Trainspotting*). The film's setting is the elegant district of Edinburgh's New Town. Three venal young buddies (David, Alex and Juliet) have set up home in an opulent Georgian apartment and are hunting out a fourth tenant to fill the spare room. A procession of eager hopefuls are interviewed, humiliated and rejected before Juliet's attention is caught by Hugo (Keith Allen), an urbane loner who claims he's writing a novel about 'a priest who dies'. Hugo is cool enough to pass the prospective-flatmate test but then, almost immediately, winds up dead in his room. At this point, as with Hitchcock's *Psycho*, the film pulls the rug out from under the unsuspecting viewer. 'When you see my character in *Shallow Grave* you think "great, here's the lead",' reckons Allen, probably the most recognizable member of the cast. 'And then he goes and dies.'

Rummaging through Hugo's possessions ('It's not every day I find a story in my own flat'), Alex discovers a Gladstone bag loaded with banknotes. After some swift soul-searching, the trio decide to keep the loot for themselves. They hack up Hugo's body and dump the bits in a makeshift grave in the woods beyond town. So far, so *noir*. Only then, of course, matters take a turn for the worse. The flatmates' shaky alliance fractures spectacularly and David holes up in the loft with the loot, drilling holes through the floor to keep an eye on the apartment's comings and goings. As Eccleston's introductory voice-over puts it: 'If you can't trust your friends, well, what then?'

Shallow Grave was shot under the banner of Macdonald's hastily formed Figment Films and put together by a team which would grow into a profitable, long-standing partnership. Alongside director Boyle and writer Hodge, cinematographer Brian Tufano and production designer Kave Quinn were also instrumental in getting the film's tone and feel just right. Both would go on to work on the subsequent collaborations, *Trainspotting* and *A Life Less Ordinary*.

Boyle had always contended that the protagonists' 'spacious, quiet, bright' flat was the movie's fourth character, and so leaned heavily on Quinn's talents. The interior, reconstructed in a warehouse on an industrial estate in Glasgow, was, at 90 by 150 feet, the biggest sound stage ever built indoors in Scottish film history; a lushly textured, perfectly functional area that Boyle's camera could traverse unobstructed.

With the finishing touches completed on set, Boyle embarked on rehearsing his players. He, Macdonald and Hodge rented a flat to share with McGregor, Fox and Eccleston, and all six camped there for over a week in August 1993. It was an unorthodox gesture; an attempt to break down the usual cloistered movie-biz environment. 'I was the one they approached first about it,' remembers Kerry Fox. 'Danny called me up and said that if I agreed to it, then it would be harder for the two boys to say no. Also I think that the British have a problem with communal living in general. They all have their things labelled in the fridge. It's so anal.'

In the end, the shared-living arrangement worked out fine. The gang sat up late going over the script. They watched videos specifically chosen to shed light on the script (Stephen Frears's pulp-*noir The Grifters*, Scorsese's *GoodFellas*, Henri-Georges Clouzot's dastardly French murder thriller *Les Diaboliques*). They invited mates over to pretend they were auditioning for a flat-share and then baited them mercilessly. Through this, Fox, Eccleston and McGregor got to know each other and learned to function as a team, all the while becoming more immersed in their characters. Boyle found this a crucial period: 'It does make you drop all the early stand-offishness you might have when you have to wait for each other to use the bathroom.' McGregor, too, looks back on the time with some nostalgia. 'That rehearsal period was brilliant from the word go,' he says. 'We used to get up, have breakfast and do scenes in our pyjamas.'

One frequent visitor, then and during the early days of the six-week shoot, was Ewan's mother. Recuperating from illness, Carol McGregor found herself on hand to witness her son's bid for glory. 'During the filming of *Shallow Grave* his mum was recovering from a breast cancer operation and he kept getting her down on set and spent all his time worrying about her,' remembers Boyle. 'It wasn't just so she could watch him, although of course she was riveted by him. He was deeply concerned that she would be all right.' Carol McGregor even bagged herself a *Shallow Grave* cameo into the bargain. She can be spotted in the opening segment playing one of the luckless losers turned down by Alex, David and Juliet.

By December, a rough-cut of the film was complete. Channel 4 took it to France to screen before the selection panel for the following spring's Cannes Film Festival where it was eventually shown out of competition in an evening market screening. Elsewhere, the movie was showered with honours. In the UK it picked up the Alexander Korda Award for Best British Film of 1994. Boyle took the Best Director nod at San Sebastian. At the Dinard Film Festival, *Shallow Grave* was named Best Film, while Fox, Eccleston and McGregor took an unprecedented three-way split of the Best Actor award.

Right from the start there was the whiff of something new about *Shallow Grave*. It is not, however, a perfect film, and in many ways shows its pedigree as the first script from an unproven writer. At times the characterization seems troubled, with abrupt tics but little linear progression. Alex, David and Juliet start out as smug, spiteful yuppies and they end up as smug, spiteful yuppies. This blunts the impact of their eventual slide into murderous backstabbing and weakens the film's move towards a *Treasure of the Sierra Madre*-type meditation on greed and friendship.

That said, Boyle's debut remains a brilliantly nasty and exciting thriller. Unlike *Shopping*, it keeps its horizons tight and doesn't reach self-consciously towards some zeitgeist-defining quality. And yet, for all that, *Shallow Grave* feels marvellously contemporary (from its speed-rush beginning, through to the bitter end) and genuinely cinematic – an accolade rarely ascribed to British cinema. Boyle makes the most of his locations and adds a few flamboyant flashes of inspiration too. Take the multiple beams of light which slice up through the drill-holes, dramatically illuminating Eccleston's loft retreat. Stylized to the nth degree, these scenes fairly brim with visual inventiveness. In helming *Shallow Grave*, Boyle broke spectacularly away from his theatrical origins.

Added to this is the fact that *Shallow Grave* is also quite startlingly amoral. Its tone conspicuously ignores the usual kitchen-sink approach to modern British milieux. Says Boyle:

> Here was a script that didn't have all the moral baggage that British films carry around all the time. *Shallow Grave* is not about class or society or people being crushed by forces they can't control. Everybody takes responsibility for their decisions. We didn't want this film to be soaked in British social realism.

Keith Allen, making amends for his role in *Beyond Bedlam*, sees *Shallow Grave* as a film of its time: 'There is a generation who like going to see things where there are no sympathetic characters. Look at the success of *Seinfeld*.'

Once again, then, America provided the inspiration. 'We've always compared it to an American independent film,' adds Boyle, 'which has a kind of energy without ramming its message down your throat. A lot of film-makers believe that if they are going to make a contemporary film it has to be *about* something; it has to be worthy.' Whatever else *Shallow Grave* is, it isn't worthy. In fact the whole film has the feel of an updated Restoration piece. Boyle details the back-sliding back-stabbing of his characters, shows how they come fantastically unstuck and views their troubles at a distance. There is no value judgement; no on-high verdict to condition the audience's response. We are left alone to navigate the film's moral minefield.

Shallow Grave played to sell-out crowds at the 1994 London Film Festival and was released nationwide the following January. From the off, business was brisk, reviews uniformally glowing ('the best British film of the year' declared *Empire* magazine, a touch prematurely). After all the false dawns and squandered promises, here, at last, was a genuinely new and entertaining home-grown product; a film that killed two birds with one stone, attaining both critical acclaim and mainstream box-office success. It seemed the only person who didn't like *Shallow Grave* was Chris Tarrant. The breakfast DJ and TV host allegedly threatened legal action over the film's use of his game show *Lose a*

Small-town inspirations : James Stewart with Donna Reed in Capra's *It's A Wonderful Life*.
© Ronald Grant

False dawns : Jude Law in *Shopping*. © Courtesy of Channel 4

.... David Thewlis in *Naked*. © Courtesy of Channel 4

Facing the future : the cast of Dennis Potter's *Lipstick on Your Collar.*
© Stephen Morley for Channel 4

McGregor in the Channel 4 short *Family Style* :
'I was so proud of that.'
© Courtesy of Channel 4

Scene of the crime : Ewan McGregor in *Shallow Grave*. © Courtesy of Channel 4

Part one of Boyle's 'bag of money' trilogy : *Shallow Grave*. © Courtesy of Channel 4

Shallow Grave : Eccleston, Fox and McGregor in interrogation mode. © Courtesy of Channel 4

Surf's up for the *Blue Juice* crew. 'It just went nowhere in the second half.' © Kobal

Northern soul : Ewan and Tara in *Brassed Off.* © Kobal

Brassed Off : McGregor with co-star Stephen Tompkinson. © Kobal

The Pillow Book : from art-house to bath-house. © Ronald Grant

Written on the body : *The Pillow Book*'s Vivian Wu. © Kobal

Million as an ironic counterpoint to the galloping avarice of *Shallow Grave*'s protagonists.

Macdonald and PolyGram (the film's distributor) had initially toyed with the idea of following the *Four Weddings and a Funeral* tactic of releasing *Shallow Grave* in the United States first, reasoning that a healthy performance there would then boomerang back on the British market in the form of fevered advance-word anticipation. In the event, the film debuted in the UK a month before its US appearance, pulling in a vibrant £553,000 in the first fortnight of release (more than half of its total budget). But if Macdonald was tilting at a transatlantic crossover success, *Shallow Grave* failed conspicuously (just as *Shopping* had before it). Despite its American-indie ambience, the film did poorly in the States, struggling to find a mainstream audience.

Meanwhile, in Europe, *Shallow Grave* performed brilliantly. All told, it took £5 million at British cinemas and £14 million worldwide. In France, particularly, the film was a huge hit, sitting for three weeks at the top of their box-office chart. This isn't so surprising when we consider the sources of the three major players' influences. Boyle, Hodge and Macdonald took their lead from the American indie film, and yet, by and large, the American–indie film took its inspiration from 1960s European cinema.

Their touchstones were the lean psychological thrillers of directors like Claude Chabrol and Jean-Pierre Melville, whose *Le Samourai*, in particular, influenced a whole host of up-and-coming indie directors (Tarantino included). *Shallow Grave*, perhaps inadvertently, simply brought the style home to this continent; a strangely roundabout form of cross-cultural pilfering. Prior to filming, Boyle had made his charges study Clouzot's *Les Diaboliques* (about a murder plot at a claustrophobic boarding school) and that film's cruel, poisonous panache is a recurrent theme in *Shallow Grave*. Small wonder the French were so enamoured of *Shallow Grave*: its gleeful, stylized fatalism came straight out of their own recent film history.

With *Shallow Grave* gearing up for release, Ewan McGregor was stuck down in Cornwall on a chilly ten-week shoot for *Blue Juice*, a *Big Wednesday*-style rites-of-passage yarn which was touted as 'Britan's first surf movie'. After *Shallow Grave*, this was, almost inevitably, a bump back down to earth. The picture was the brain-child of writer–director Carl Prechezer and writer–producer Peter Salmi, who had hooked up at the Royal College of Art and shared a desire 'to make big films for big audiences'. Their debut told the tale of JC (*Shopping* baddie Sean Pertwee), a hot-shot surfer pushing thirty and badgered by his girlfriend (Catherine Zeta Jones) to settle down and abandon his beach-bum lifestyle.

McGregor – as yet not riding the *Shallow Grave* crest – contented himself with a support role. He plays Dean, a scuzzball dope-dealer who doubles, implausibly, as a stringer for the tabloids. Or as Ewan puts it: 'He's a sad person, a complete loser with no job, no skills, and he sells drugs in London and he's not even good at that.' The film went before the cameras in September 1994 at locations around St Ives, with the four leading actors (Sean Pertwee, Peter Gunn, Steven Mackintosh and Ewan McGregor) getting on-the-spot training from expert surfers Rob Small and Steve England (who also served in the film as stunt doubles). The film was bracingly shot by cinematographer Richard Greatrex and boasted a few nice comic touches, but overall *Blue Juice* proved to be a weak and woolly yarn.

Released in the autumn of 1995, Prechezer's film fell flat in a domestic scene suddenly re-energized by *Shallow Grave*'s arrival. It looked like a postcard from a bygone age. Heartfelt and occasionally charming it may have been, but it also came over as faintly outmoded, near clumsy in its blend of old-fashioned structures (the traditional comedy) with voguish, youthful trappings. Today McGregor looks back on *Blue Juice* with some regret. 'I had a great time making it and was really happy with the work that I did on it, but there was something wrong with the script. It just went nowhere in the second half, and actually became quite boring.' Even so, he could walk away with his head held high. In a kind review of *Blue Juice* by trade Bible *Variety* magazine, McGregor was reckoned to have 'delivered the pic's best performance as bordering-on-psycho Dean'. Once again, the Ewan factor – emerging from a wobbly project with his dignity intact – had come to the rescue. It had first worked in that long-ago church production of *David and Goliath* in Crieff. Now McGregor was applying the gift to the cut-and-thrust world of mainstream movie-making.

It was *Shallow Grave*, though, that really turned McGregor's career around. Boyle's debut became the year's highest-grossing British film in the UK. Its success alone raised McGregor's profile a hundredfold, lifting him above the ranks of the other British acting hopefuls. More importantly, *Shallow Grave*'s success found McGregor indelibly associated with a new brand of British cinema. As opposed to co-stars Christopher Eccleston and Kerry Fox, McGregor came to the project untainted by past mistakes, unshackled to previous schools of film-making or well-known previous pictures. His experience was limited to two years of TV and one blink-and-you'll-miss-him debut in a straight-to-video feature. He was an actor without baggage who was fresh and new. When all is said and done, *Shallow Grave* was his real movie debut.

What remained to be seen was how McGregor might build on this success; whether the Boyle–Macdonald–Hodge team would continue; and whether, if so, there was a place for Ewan in their ongoing collaborations. On the face it, the Figment Films production team looked an unlikely alliance: a thirtysomething TV veteran, a young tyro producer of film-making lineage and a medical Scot who, after finishing his script, had returned to working as a locum at a south London hospital. John Hodge, in particular, gave the impression that he was only in for the short haul. During *Shallow Grave*'s first giddy cinema run, he lamented:

> I miss working at the hospital when I'm not there. I don't miss staying up all night but the human contact. I don't want to write screenplays for the rest of my life. I would get bored with the film industry. I feel I only have three or four scripts in me.

Hodge claims that after *Shallow Grave* he even considered calling it quits altogether; getting out of the writing game while the going was good. Yet this sounds disingenuous. As early as January 1995 the team already had their next two features mapped out. They wanted to stay independent; they wanted to remain working as a unit. On the cards, they said, was a film based on another original script by Hodge: a romantic-comedy set in the States which went by the name of *A Life Less Ordinary*. First, though, the team planned to turn their hand to an altogether different project.

In February 1994, with *Shallow Grave* still in post-production, Macdonald had visited Hodge with a book he thought might make a decent film. The doctor, for his part, wasn't sure. At first glance, Irvine Welsh's *Trainspotting* appeared unfilmable. It was dense and impenetrable, its narrative at times verging on stream-of-consciousness. Where other novels followed a linear flow that could translate simply into a filmic three-act structure, Welsh's book sprawled all over the place. It was, Hodge decided, less a novel and more a scattered and shattered series of episodes; a splash of loosely linked set-pieces brought together by one unifying theme – the heroin culture of inner-city Edinburgh. Crafting this slippery customer into a usable screenplay was to mark Hodge's coming of age as a writer.

TRAINSPOTTING

4. TRAINSPOTTING

Pick any major actor of the past thirty years and there is usually that key moment, that iconic introduction in some breakthrough film that announces their arrival, that somehow lifts them above the dictates of plot and character and sets them apart. For the young, skinny Robert De Niro, it came in the opening minutes of *Mean Streets*, ushered in slow-motion through a busy bar as the Rolling Stones' 'Jumping Jack Flash' revved up in the background. For Dustin Hoffman, it was a passive profile shot at the start of *The Graduate*, Simon and Garfunkel's 'The Sound of Silence' tinkling on the soundtrack. To all intents and purposes, Ewan McGregor – the movie star as opposed to the film actor – was played in to the dustbin-lid clatter of Iggy Pop's 'Lust for Life'. We see a blur of legs in drainpipe jeans, a flurry of discarded items littering the street behind him and then the first good look at his face – crop-haired, bony – grinning dementedly through the windshield of the car that knocks him down. The image seems self-consciously significant. Our point of view is with the car's driver, looking from the outside in. What follows tugs us through to the windshield's other side, pulls us right into the heart of *Trainspotting*'s junkie subculture.

A few days before Christmas 1993, with *Shallow Grave* in post-production, Andrew Macdonald boarded a flight from London to Glasgow and found himself engrossed in a book a friend had recommended. Irvine Welsh's *Trainspotting* had been in bookshops for nearly a year, its sales buoyed by reviews which hailed it as a landmark novel, a shattering exposé of the heroin scene thriving in Edinburgh's depressed district of Leith. For Welsh it seemed simple. Drug-use, he felt, was the great unspoken component of modern life: the wellspring of youth culture. 'Anybody who writes a book set in Britain today with no reference to drugs', he reckoned, 'is living in total never-never land.'

Certainly Welsh's approach boasted crucial differences to the one-step-removed decadence of contemporaries like Martin Amis and Will Self: both confessed drug-users but middle class, Oxbridge educated and with iron-clad connections to London's media scene. By contrast, the Scotsman's warts-and-all immediacy and impenetrable regional dialect stuck in close to its subject matter while daring the reader to follow suit. Born into working-class Edinburgh, Welsh initially began writing as a form of self-service, to provide himself with the sort of material he wanted to read but could never find. He would later deny all liter-ary influences, claiming that Richard Allen's culty seventies *Skinhead* books were the only novels he ever got off on:

> I wanted to read about characters I could identify with and the club scene, with its constant action . . . I thought I could do something better. People think I've this big intellectual pose but it's anything but that. You pick up any novel in Britain and it's the same narrative voice. Literary fiction in Britain is so similar it's become genre fiction, like crime writing or sci-fi.

Written in 1992, *Trainspotting* threw a loose canopy across the heroin highs and cold-turkey lows of a crop of Edinburgh junkies. Its plot was fused by the experiences of these characters. Its stark cluster of episodes mapped out a culture rarely captured in such a non-judgemental fashion and presented a literary examination of drug use which ranked alongside William Burroughs's *Junkie* and Huxley's *The Doors of Perception*. Pitched somewhere in the sky between Glasgow and London, Andrew Macdonald was hooked:

> I'm not a great reader – I don't read many novels at all – but I was really bowled over by this book . . . This was not some voyeuristic Oxford graduate's perception of these people. It really felt like it was written from within, in a completely unsentimental way.

In truth, Macdonald was not the first to spot *Trainspotting*'s cinema potential. The book was already being considered for a possible film adaptation, but Welsh had tenaciously clung on to the rights, reluctant to let his baby go and unconvinced by the outlook of the cinema big-wigs he had encountered:

> Just talking to them, I could see they wanted to turn it into some dull and worthy bit of social-realism . . . An important picture nobody wants to see is ultimately just a self-important picture that nobody wants to see.

Macdonald, meantime, was determined to make *Trainspotting* the team's next project. He stressed the relevance of Hodge's and his own Scottish roots and Danny Boyle was given the task of writing an introductory letter to Welsh which boasted that the writer–producer pair were 'the two most important Scotsmen since Kenny Dalglish and Alex Ferguson'. Such peacock swaggering went down well with Welsh, a literary outsider who wore his suspicions of London's movers and shakers like a badge of honour. He met with the trio and agreed to let the rights go. What he didn't want, he told them, was 'the Ken

Loach, social-documentary approach. It has to have energy and action.' Happily, the *Shallow Grave* team wanted that too. From that moment on, *Trainspotting* was officially in development.

Even so, the difficulties involved in shunting the production on towards completion were monumental. For a start, Welsh's anecdotal narrative vigorously resisted anything so straightforward as a standard three-act movie adaptation. Furthermore, the subject matter was volatile. Drug use had been covered in mainstream cinema before, of course, most contentiously in Otto Preminger's fifties drama *The Man with the Golden Arm*, which showcased Frank Sinatra as a smack-addict jazz musician. But, by and large, drug-themed pictures circumvented the censor by adopting a distanced and didactic stance. The emphasis was on drug abuse as opposed to drug use. The counter-culture time-piece *Easy Rider*, from 1969, broke a taboo of sorts by revelling in the upsides of marijuana and LSD, while more fringe film-makers like Kenneth Anger and Andy Warhol pushed drug use to the forefront of their own decadent, idiosyncratic visions. In the late eighties, Gus Van Sant's undervalued indie outing *Drugstore Cowboy* followed the Preminger tack by turning its attention to heroin, showing the up-sides of star Matt Dillon's junkie existence before revealing the meandering drift towards death that is invariably the long-term addict's eventual lot in life. Meanwhile, in the UK, specifically drug-themed films remained all but non-existent.

Ironically it was the rise of Ecstasy as opposed to heroin which made a picture on the scale of *Trainspotting* a viable possibility. For where heroin was stigmatized as a predominantly underclass drug, Ecstasy, which made its first appearance in the clublands of Manchester and London in the late 1980s, thrived among the young and middle class. Its arrival re-energized a club scene which had been winding down since the days of disco. Ecstasy was a 'trendy' drug, intrinsically bound up in dance music and youth culture. Subsequently it drew more sustained and concentrated media attention than heroin had ever provoked.

In 1996, the year of *Trainspotting*'s release, a survey for the *Independent on Sunday* discovered that 67 per cent of young people (with an average age of nineteen) had taken an illegal drug within the previous six months, and 53 per cent of children would have experimented with drugs before leaving school. More importantly, suveys showed that recreational drug use was a shade higher in affluent areas than in its traditional inner-city stomping ground. For the tabloids, such figures were cause for widespread hysteria. For others, they confirmed that drug use was a fact of life in modern-day Britain, a trend no longer confined to the social and economic underclass.

In a sense, then, Welsh's novel was a book out of time. Welsh once admitted that *Trainspotting*'s time-scale was the mid- to late eighties, when heroin use was at its high-water mark in the cities of Scotland. The gap between the two cultures was pronounced: where Ecstasy resonated across the class system, heroin typically flourished amid the urban poor. And where the Ecstasy scene tended to be vibrant and inclusive, heroin culture was invariably self-contained and clandestine. Yet, for all that, the one paved the way for a film dealing with the other. The sudden focus on Ecstasy (in particular) ushered drug use (in general) into the public arena. From the start, Andrew Macdonald's second feature was ideally positioned to tap into the mood of the age.

In the entire spectrum of illegal narcotics, heroin occupied the darkest peripheries. In bald statistical terms, its initial impact looks slight. While cannabis is responsible for 80 per cent of seizures and convictions in the UK, heroin accounts for only 5 per cent. Yet within its niche, this is a serious phenomenon. In his 1998 study *Drugs and the Party Line*, Kevin Williamson reports that heroin accounts for no less than 90 per cent of registered drug addicts in Britain. By 1991 it was estimated that there were over 120,000 heroin addicts in the UK, with a hard-core population concentrated in the impoverished estates of Glasgow and Edinburgh. It was this world that Welsh's novel targeted.

Not that his tale was unremittingly grim. On the contrary, *Trainspotting* tempered its topic with an edge of vitality, wit and ingenuity. It took its rogues' gallery of characters and gave them the flesh and blood bulk of truth. Rather than grey case-studies in a social report, *Trainspotting*'s fraternity of Edinburgh wastrels fairly bristled with life. The book traces their experiences, acknowledges both the pros and cons of heroin use and was written from the inside-out in a determinedly non-preachy style. So while *Trainspotting* conformed in many ways to the traditional tenets of social realism, in that it alerted its readers to a harrowing aspect of British culture, it drew the line pushing any pre-packed message. Readers were left to draw their own conclusions. 'What appealed to me was the surrealistic style of it,' said Macdonald, 'the way it refuses to conform to social realism, which as a genre is one of my pet hates.'

Danny Boyle agreed:

> Social realism's objective eye creates victims. I don't know what value showing that has any more. We've moved on from social welfare in Britain when it was useful to identify victims. We collectively decided – and we elected Thatcher for twelve years to do it – that we don't want to do that any more. We've moved away from the great post-war ideal that we can be communal.

All of which gave Boyle's *Trainspotting* a strange pedigree. Here was a film that exposed society's fall-out and implicitly damned the Thatcher legacy, yet did so through an aesthetic stance that was boldly Thatcherite in tone. It was a film of and for its time.

Nonetheless, some observers were still bewildered by the team's decision to go with so potentially dispiriting and gritty a tale. In a meeting with Macdonald shortly after *Shallow Grave*'s release, *Chariots of Fire* producer David Puttnam apparently urged Macdonald to reconsider, arguing that a film about junkies in Edinburgh was both box-office suicide and a reductive retreat into glum, socially conscious British drama. Macdonald, Puttnam felt, should capitalize on his present success to make a still bigger, brighter picture with the widest possible audience base. 'After the success of *Shallow Grave* we were offered a suitcase full of cash by Hollywood,' recalls Macdonald. 'But we felt it was important to stay in London and make another contemporary film. *Trainspotting* fitted the bill – even if it meant cutting the fees to work on a Channel 4 budget.' After David Aukin had been so instrumental in getting *Shallow Grave* off the ground, Macdonald felt he owed Channel 4 first refusal on *Trainspotting*. While a step up from the team's debut, the budget was still minute (£1.7 million). Aided by *Shallow Grave*'s reception, Channel 4 had no difficulty in pre-selling the project around the world.

The first proper steps were taken in the spring of 1994. Taking a break from hospital work, Hodge joined Macdonald and Boyle on a fact-finding mission to the Edinburgh suburb of Leith. It was at this point that the film experienced its first major hiccups. While Welsh's protagonists were vital underdogs who struggled in their idiosyncratic ways to get a handle on their drug use, the Leith junkies encountered by Boyle and the team were mired deep in an addiction so advanced that there was probably little chance of a turnaround. Where Welsh's book posed questions and explored the appeal of heroin before depicting its down-side, the Leith junkies offered the film-makers no such perspective. 'We met a lot of guys who were pretty sad addicts, who weren't in recovery, who were using it,' says Boyle. 'To be honest, when we came away from these places, we said "People won't want to see a film about these guys." '

To find an artistic stance on heroin use, the film-makers had to drop back from the front line and discuss the culture with those who had a first-hand acquaintance with the drug and yet were now 'clean' and more objective regarding its effects. From Leith, the team moved west to meet with workers and intakes at the Calton Athletic Drug Rehabilitation Centre in Glasgow. In terms of research, this was like striking gold. Initially founded as a football club for ex-junkies, Calton broke with the widespread policy of prescribing methadone to heroin users. Founder David Bryce felt the methadone approach merely ties users into another pattern of addiction. It was, he argued, a 'tragic and defeatist' means to combat heroin abuse. Intakes at the Calton Athletic Club, on the other hand, underwent withdrawal in a managed, supportive environment and in the company of trained drugs workers and other recovering users. Boyle dubbed them 'fanatical abstainers. To meet them you get that feeling of seeing life again in people who have been away from us.' Macdonald agreed: 'They were a great inspiration to us. Not only in an abstract way, they also became our guides through drug culture; explaining and demonstrating for us.' Calton, then, was to play a crucial role in translating Welsh's novel to the screen.

John Hodge was to play another. With *Trainspotting* in the early stages of development, Macdonald had toyed with the idea of having Welsh adapt the novel himself, or at least collaborate with Hodge on the screenplay. Welsh, however, was not interested. He felt he had already told the story and had since moved on to other projects. He had no particular wish to revisit the landscape and people of Leith. So the job fell entirely to Hodge. His script for *Trainspotting* went through four drafts, each one interspersed with lengthy consultations with Macdonald. It was a gargantuan piece of tailoring. Certain scenes were lost for good (including Hodge's favourite chapter, 'Memories of Matty'). Others were built up, reordered and restructured, to give a proper narrative thrust to the tale. Welsh's 'choose life' mantra was shunted to the front of the story, to become both a piquant introduction and the film's dominating ethos. In the meantime, Hodge inserted some dialogue of his own. A football fan, he was particularly pleased to have sneaked in Renton's post-sex reference to Scottish striker Archie Gemmill ('I haven't felt that good since Archie Gemmill scored against Holland in 1978'). Welsh, though, was not entirely without his say. He provided Hodge with various suggestions and a few criticisms which contributed to the finished version.

By December 1994 a working screenplay was in place. It was not Welsh's *Trainspotting* – the tone had been lightened a shade; the rash of incidents herded into one narrative line. But the book's energy and spirit lingered on every page. Hodge's script for *Shallow Grave* provided a decent foundation for a new type of British film, but it was, of itself, not particularly innovative. This screenplay, with its blend of looseness and urgency, its playful fringes and harrowing interiors, was revolutionary. By taking Welsh's novel as a starting point, Hodge had come up with something that was both true to the original text yet very much his own work. When all is said and done, *Trainspotting* was his masterpiece.

It was, too, an impeccably lean and trim affair, a script without an ounce of extra fat or self-indulgence. During the golden age of Motown there was a semi-serious school of thought that reckoned the perfect pop song ran at precisely two minutes and fifty-eight seconds. For his part, Macdonald was determined that, in order to maintain its hard, fast trajectory, *Trainspotting* should not run over ninety minutes. He, Boyle and Hodge held firm to the rule. The film's finished print cuts out on the dot of eighty-nine minutes.

The blueprint in place, the next stage was filling in the gaps. At the heart of Welsh's tale sits Renton, the swaggering, smack-addled anti-hero whose back-sliding attempts to go straight litter the novel. Hodge's script had brought Renton still further to the fore of the narrative and made him more of an every-man figure – the anchor that holds the script in place and strikes a balance with the more lurid extravagances of the characters who surround him. Boyle and Macdonald still had no idea who they wanted for the supporting roles. But from the earliest days of *Trainspotting*'s conception, Ewan McGregor was earmarked for the role of Renton. Only John Hodge was doubtful; concerned that McGregor's easy, middle-class air wasn't right for the part. But Boyle and Macdonald overrode him. There was but one condition. 'Ewan was the logical choice so long as he was prepared to lose weight,' reckons Boyle. 'Because he's normally quite a chunky fellow. He said, "I'll do it", and he fucked off, and six weeks later he walked in and he was like a stick.'

McGregor was shown the script in January 1995 and embarked on a customized diet to attain the wippy, malnourished look that was crucial for Renton. In this he was helped by girlfriend Eve (pronounced 'Ev') Mavrakis, a Parisian production designer he had met a few months earlier while playing a rapist in the first episode of the John Thaw legal potboiler *Kavanagh QC*. 'Was it love at first sight? Yeah, I suppose it was actually,' says McGregor. 'I remember very clearly thinking that if I could be with this person everything would be OK in my life. After filming was over we kind of chased each other around London for a bit and then got together and that was that.' Five years McGregor's senior, Mavrakis became something of a stabilizer on the actor's lifestyle, and her arrival brought down the curtain on McGregor's single life: an existence centred on his bachelor pad in Primrose Hill. 'The things that went on there,' he recalls. 'But in the end it all got a bit depressing.' In fact, the Mavrakis relationship followed a liaison with another French woman, production manager Marie Pairis, on the set of *Scarlet and Black*. 'French women are difficult,' he explains. 'And I like difficult women.'

During the run-up to *Trainspotting*, Eve doubled as 'my nutritionist. She worked out this diet for me where we just grilled everything we ate. And I stopped drinking beer and started drinking wine and plenty of gin, which wasn't too bad. The weight just fell off.' McGregor shed twenty four pounds to reach a fighting weight of ten stone.

As an example of physical make-over, this hardly rivals Robert De Niro's Method approach when making *Raging Bull* (while filming stopped for two months, De Niro piled on fifty pounds to play boxer Jake La Motta in bloated, broken-down middle age), but it was still hugely impressive. Compare *Trainspotting*'s McGregor with the *Shallow Grave* version and it's almost like seeing a different person. The puppy fat is gone; the planes and angles of his face stand out in stark repose; the thick, back-swept hair is replaced with a blunt, buzz-saw cut. For fans of the book (including Hodge) wary of a deodorized, Hollywood-style treatment, the mere sight of the new, pared-down McGregor must have allayed a lot of fears.

That said, McGregor hardly looked the archetypal junkie (assuming, of course, that an archetypal junkie is what Renton is meant to be). In some quarters there was disappointment that Boyle and Macdonald didn't risk offering the lead role to Ewen Bremner. Certainly Bremner, with his slouching frame and hang-dog looks, more fitted the aesthetic of the deadbeat smack addict. More importantly, he had a proven track record, having already played Renton on stage in an acclaimed theatre adaptation for the best part of a year. Yet, in cinematic terms, Bremner remained a box-office virgin. More crucial, one suspects, was the sex angle. McGregor was always destined to make the more obviously attractive lead, and the rejection of Bremner is one of the few aspects of *Trainspotting*'s production that bears the faint whiff of Hollywood-style compromise.

Bremner made do with a second-string role as Spud, the shambling, genial junkie who becomes the tale's most overtly comic and sympathetic figure. 'Which was OK,' he says philosophically. 'I felt that I'd already done Renton anyway, and I wasn't even sure I'd have wanted to play him again. You get a bit sick of being in somebody's skin for a whole year. I think that's a natural response.' Welsh's story, though, still intrigued him. 'I felt that these characters were part of my heritage. I'm from Portobello, which is only a couple of miles from Leith, where *Trainspotting* is set. I grew up surrounded by that world.'

For the role of Sick Boy, Renton's suave, Sean Connery-obsessed partner in crime, the makers hit on twenty-two-year-old Jonny Lee Miller. At the time of casting, Miller was just completing work on *Hackers*, a cartoonish computer thriller from director Iain Softley, who had earlier made his name with the John Lennon–Stuart Sutcliffe biopic *Backbeat*. On *Hackers*, Miller sported a wavering New York accent and wound up marrying his co-star, Angelina Jolie, daughter of *Midnight Cowboy* star John Voight. As an acting showcase, *Hackers* looked tawdry, though Miller made instant amends at his first meeting with Boyle and

Macdonald by slipping into a pitch-pefect impression of Connery's throaty drawl. In fact, Miller's connection to the Bond films went further than impeccable mimicry. His grandfather was the late Bernard Lee, who had played Secret Service boss 'M' in twelve 007 outings.

Tommy, the clean living steady-Eddie who drifts into drug abuse, was played by newcomer Kevin McKidd. He had just finished working on Gillies MacKinnon's fine Glasgow rites-of-passage drama *Small Faces*, in which he had played a hulking, vicious gang leader, yet Boyle spotted in him a clear-eyed inno-cence (which he likened to 'meeting the Beach Boys at the height of their fame') that seemed right for Tommy. For Diane, the nymphet night-clubber who takes charge of Renton, Boyle arranged an open audition. Flyers were distributed around Glasgow and over 200 hopefuls showed up on the day. Boyle went with the unknown Kelly Macdonald, who was eighteen but could pass for four years younger. 'As soon as Kelly sat down,' he said, 'I knew it should be her.' For the other female vacancies (whose roles had been beefed up from the novel), Shirley Anderson stepped in as Spud's girlfriend Gail and *Naked* actress Susan Vidler appeared as junkie mum Allison.

Begbie posed more of a problem. He was *Trainspotting*'s Grendel: the monstrous, pub-brawling blow-hard whom the gang are terrified of and yet never quite manage to shake off. Or, as Tommy puts it, 'The Beggar is fucking psycho, but he's a mate, you know, so what can you do?' Reading both the book and Hodge's treatment, Boyle and Macdonald naturally envisaged Begbie as some brawny, endomorphic lout. Eager to preserve the *Shallow Grave* team, Macdonald initially wanted Christopher Eccleston for the role. When Eccleston proved to be doubtful in terms of both scheduling and desire, other options were hastily considered. During these discussions, producer and director hit on the notion that Begbie should be a smaller man: a compact, moustachioed pitbull perpetually buzzing with nervous energy, forever desperate to prove himself to the world at large.

The role of Begbie – in many respects the peach part in *Trainspotting* – was offered to Robert Carlyle. Macdonald half-expected his offer of the part to be turned down, but the book had already struck a chord with the Scottish-born actor. 'I've met loads of Begbies in my time,' Carlyle says. 'Wander around Glasgow on a Saturday night and you've a good chance of running into Begbie.' But, he added, 'Begbie didn't seem to be the obvious part for me. I'd seen him being six-foot-five in all directions. But, as Danny Boyle said, "small psychos are the best".'

It was the novel, though, that really snagged Carlyle's interest: 'It was very easy for me to relate to the world of the film. The estate I was brought up on in Glasgow was the Glaswegian equivalent of Leith. A lot of guys from my genera-tion – some of my friends – got involved in the drug scene.' Not that Begbie is a heroin user himself, of course. 'No way would I poison my body wi' that shite; all they fucking chemicals' he quips, between bolting his shot of Scotch while a fag smoulders in the ashtray at his side.

With the arrival of Carlyle, *Trainspotting*'s crucial cast dynamic was in place: loose, easy McGregor on one side, jittery, turbulent Carlyle on the other. In its own peculiar way, this double-header evoked memories of Newman and Redford in *Butch Cassidy and the Sundance Kid*; or De Niro and Keitel in *Mean Streets*. Two of the era's finest up-and-comers in a film that showcased their respective talents. For if McGregor has a genuine rival in the current British film landscape, it can only be Robert Carlyle, as his later success in *The Full Monty* would show. Ironically, both actors had screen-tested for the part of Alex in *Shallow Grave*. McGregor won the role, but the rejection was to prove a mere blip on Carlyle's CV.

Thirty-four at the time of shooting, Carlyle is McGregor's senior by ten years. And while Ewan's career hit a high note from his very first acting job, Carlyle has trodden a longer, more arduous route. Raised amid the hippy communes of Glasgow's Maryhill district by his painter-decorator dad, Carlyle flunked out of school with no qualifications, helped his father out for a time and then fell into acting almost by accident. He set up his own theatre company, Rain Dog, in 1986 (named after the classic Tom Waits album of the previous year), but found regular work tough to come by. When he travelled to the Cannes Film Festival in 1990, to promote Ken Loach's *Riff-Raff* (in which he played a shy building-site labourer), it was the first time Carlyle had ever been abroad.

After *Riff-Raff*, Carlyle steered a steadier course. He was a manic serial killer in TV's *Cracker*, a dreadlocked self-abuser in Antonia Bird's homeless saga *Safe* and the gay lover of Linus Roache's cleric in 1994's *Priest*, also directed by Bird. Following the success of *Priest*, Carlyle was wooed by Hollywood. In the event, he stayed true to his determination to take on challenging, authentic roles in British cinema, turning down roles in both *Rob Roy* and the Oscar-winning *Braveheart*. 'I wasn't into being a hairy-arsed Highlander charging up a hill,' he shrugged. Carlyle's pre-shoot homework verged on the fanatical. Before appearing in *Safe* he had camped out, penniless, on the streets around Waterloo Station for a week, mixing with the down-and-outs and plucking his food from the dustbins outside a nearby McDonald's.

Playing Begbie, Carlyle seemed to sink into the role to an unnerving degree. Electing to interpret Welsh's character as 'a kind of homosexual Ian Rush', he pursed his lips below a bristly moustache and swaggered around in 'casual' fashions: Pringle pullies, gold jewellery glinting at his throat and wrists, and gleaming white socks ('the badge of the nutter,' Carlyle points out). The effect, so close to being comic, was all the more scary for it. Boyle recounts a tale of when the crew were shooting the notorious pint-slopping scene that comes near the film's close. Boyle was shooting the extras' reactions first but found them blank and unresponsive, scarcely communicating any of the terror required of them. Carlyle took Boyle aside. 'Let me do my bit first and then film them,' he told the director. Boyle rearranged the set and the actor launched into his act while Boyle shot the extras; all suddenly, shockingly afraid. The amphetamined fury of Begbie even took its creator aback. 'That was the first time in my whole career that I've been surprised with the final result,' Carlyle says. 'There's something in the eyes that I didn't know was there on the day. Fucking worrying, really.'

McGregor, meantime, was getting accustomed to Renton. Prior to filming he waded through various books on heroin addiction. The early months of 1995 found him in Luxembourg, filming sections of Peter Greenaway's erotic art-house fable *The Pillow Book*. Junkies congregated at the railway terminal and during his time off from filming, McGregor would take himself down there, studying their appearance, their bearing, the way they interacted. 'I would go there on Sundays,' he recalls. 'I got some of my look from them and some of my physical ideas. For example, in one of the first scenes I used this particularly stooped posture for Renton which is an exact rip-off of a guy I saw in Luxembourg.'

Boyle, too, was obsessed with finding the perfect look for *Trainspotting*. He studied the twisted, anguished paintings of Francisco Goya, Francis Bacon and Egon Schiele and put together a scrapbook of pictures which caught the disorientating, dislocated essence he was hunting for: 'Lots of very low and very high angles, lots of feet and leg shots.' A derelict cigarette factory on the edge of Glasgow proved a boon for production designer Kave Quinn. Thirty of the film's fifty locations were shot there, and it was Quinn's task to dress these sets, to make the interiors mirror the characters' own troubled states. Tommy's flat, for instance, grows more dank and decayed as the character turns gradually sicker. 'Francis Bacon's colours were particularly influential,' Quinn says. 'His paintings represent a sort of in-between land – part reality, part fantasy – which seemed very *Trainspotting* to me.'

Before filming began, Boyle and his cast holed up for a time with the recovering addicts from the Calton Athletic Club. Eamon Docherty, in particular, became the team's chief mentor. A heroin addict since the age of fourteen, Docherty had been clean for four years and served as *Trainspotting*'s 'technical adviser'. On-set, he conducted 'cookery classes' for the actors and tutored them in the practicalities of heroin use. 'We were each given about five needles and all the paraphernalia for shooting up, and we had to practise until we did it right,' says Kevin McKidd. 'The guy marched up and down telling us what we were doing wrong. He'd go, "OK, do this, don't do that, make sure you put the water around the powder rather than squirting it on the powder." He came round and he marked us all on it. It was just like Bruce Forsyth's *Generation Game*.'

Boyle, apparently, became so immersed in *Trainspotting*'s homework that he claims, surely half in jest, that he even toyed with the notion of shooting up alongside other actors and crew members. But, he says, 'we decided not to in the end'. McGregor claims to have experienced the same dilemma:

> I thought about actually taking heroin, and the more research I did, the less I wanted to do it. I didn't think it was necessary. I've had to die on screen before, and I don't know what that's like either. I'm not a Method actor at all, so to take heroin for the part would just be an excuse to take heroin. So I didn't.

Yet far from dampening the speculation, such remarks gave rise to rumours of actors and crew getting too close to their material; of dangerously blurring the lines between art and reality. Those rumours have lingered, in low-key, whispered form, right through to the present day.

Away from their addict classes, the cast hung out socially with the Calton crowd. Soccer, for a time, became a serious diversion. The footballers featured in the film's intro are all Calton intakes, a fit, committed bunch who put the actors to shame. 'We couldn't believe they were recovering addicts,' says McGregor. 'They were running circles around us and we were all coughing up our last cigarettes.' This would not be disputed by the Calton sportsmen, who considered McGregor a patchy footballer and Ewen Bremner even worse.

Trainspotting went before the cameras on 22 May 1995 and continued through an exhaustive seven-week shoot. McGregor, who is on screen virtually throughout the entire movie, had but two afternoons off. 'It was a slog for me,' he recalls. 'I was on set from morning to night, but I loved every minute of it.'

Others, though, remember McGregor as having difficulties with the role. The problems arose with how best to energize Renton, who emerged from Hodge's script as more a neutral observer than a proactive protagonist. For much of the film he sits in the centre as the action revolves around him; serving as the mediator between audience and material, in much the same way that Martin Sheen's Willard worked throughout Francis Coppola's *Apocalypse Now*. 'There's a lot of him that just goes along passively with what everyone else is doing,' McGregor admits.

> Renton is often observing. In a lot of scenes I don't have an awful lot to do physically, but at the same time he almost always has a critical edge about things in his mind which is expressed in the voice-over which runs through the film.

Some crew members remember panicked conversations between the actor and director as McGregor tried to find a centre to Renton's character. 'Well, yeah, I had my moments,' McGregor explains. 'I think every actor does. I wasn't sure exactly if I was communicating anything at all, just standing there looking like an arsehole. But Danny was fine with it. He said it would all come out right in the wash.'

Boyle, though, was putting a brave face on it. As the crew ploughed further into the seven-week shoot, rushes from the earlier days were coming back to them. Boyle would hole up in his hotel room each night and study the evidence. The outlook was not good. Even though Hodge had laboured hard to give Welsh's book a proper backbone, the film still looked too jumbled and sprawling. 'I remember feeling that it was difficult to get a hold on it,' Boyle says. 'It was so fragmented and there's not much story.'

What there was, even in those panicked pre-edit days, was a cluster of dazzling incidents. Two years on, many of *Trainspotting*'s scenes have already become iconic. Ewen Bremner's Spud covers his girlfriend's family with shit from his sheets (oxtail soup doubling as excrement). Renton undergoes horrible, hallucinatory withdrawal in the cramped single bed at his parents' home. An identikit Yankee tourist blunders blithely into a grotty Edinburgh pub and straight into Begbie's clutches. Renton delves inside a bunged-up toilet bowl to retrieve his suppository before gliding off through a fantastical under-water world. 'All that underwater stuff was great,' enthuses McGregor, who spent a day shooting the scene. 'Just because of that scene I want to do *The Abyss II*.'

At the other end of the spectrum lies Renton's overdose, sliding down into a funereal red carpet as Lou Reed's 'Perfect Day' lilts atmospherically on the soundtrack. Or the infamous dead baby episode, in which Allison's infant is left languishing, chill and blue in its crib, as his mother mainlines obliviously in an adjacent room. 'I hadn't seen the model of the dead baby before,' remembers Susan Vidler, who plays Allison. 'I'd been working with the twins who were playing the little baby and got to know them quite well – and suddenly you see a model of them looking dead. It was very nasty. Oh God, it was really horrible.'

Among the cameo cast, early morning TV host Dale Winton cropped up to give a lurid pastiche of his game-show persona, while Keith Allen (late of *Shallow Grave*) gave a brief but coolly effective turn as the big-time London criminal with whom the gang trades near the film's finale. Even Irvine Welsh was on hand, playing drug-dealer Mikey Forrester. 'It came as no surprise, being asked to do that,' laughs Welsh. 'It's a sure-fire way to spike an author's guns. Very canny indeed. I can't moan about the film and say, "Oh, they've ruined my book," because I'm fucking in it.'

As it happened, few of those involved would regret being connected with *Trainspotting*. Ultimately, McGregor and Boyle's concerns were to prove unfounded. In the editing process, running through the autumn of 1995, the film fitted together as sweetly as a nut. *Trainspotting* swung between gritty naturalism and surreal flamboyance, between chic style-piece and gruelling exposé, and yet all the while maintained a wholeness and integrity that aston-ished. This was, in short, the film the British cinema scene had been waiting for. A few weeks prior to release, McGregor speculated as to the possible reaction to his movie:

> I am heartily sick of all this cynicism and bollocks sophistication we get in Britain today. What I hope is that when *Trainspotting* comes out, people can just sit back for a bit and say, "This is just a fucking great film." No more, no less.

Some hope. *Trainspotting* was too complex, too tangled, too loaded with implication to get passed over so lightly. The film had just been completed. The resulting media storm had yet to begin.

TRAINSPOTTING ARRIVES

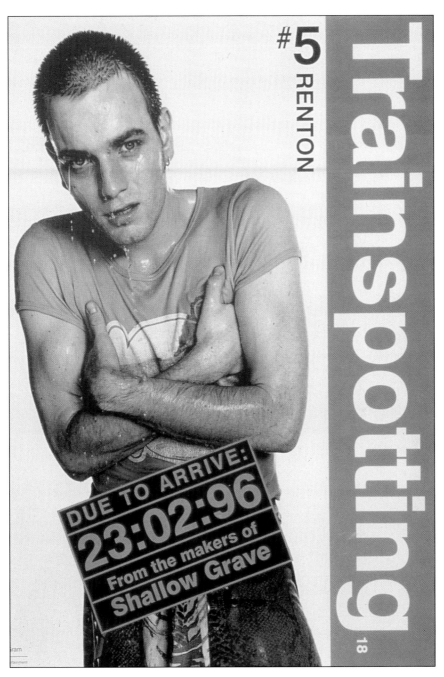

Five easy pieces ... The *Trainspotting* marketing kit. © PolyGram/Pictorial Press

The usual suspects : Bremner, Carlyle, McGregor and Miller. © PolyGram/Pictorial Press

Begbie and Renton – a marriage made in hell. © PolyGram/Pictorial Press

The drugs don't work : *Trainspotting*'s Renton laid low. © PolyGram/Pictorial Press

French cheese : McGregor and Rachel Weisz in the frolicking *Scarlet and Black*.
© BBC Picture Archives

Flipping his wig over *Emma* : 'I can't even watch myself in that one.' © Capital Pictures

Off the road in *A Life Less Ordinary*. © PolyGram/Pictorial Press

A Life Less Ordinary : Robert makes a break for it. © PolyGram/Pictorial Press

A Life Less Ordinary : line 'em up ... © PolyGram/Pictorial Press

... and knock 'em down. © PolyGram/Pictorial Press

Lady Saliva ... Robert gets his big screen kiss. © PolyGram/Pictorial Press

5. TRAINSPOTTING ARRIVES

At heart *Trainspotting* is a picaresque film: a hard, barbed, darkly comic tale; a rogues' odyssey through modern-day Britain. 'It's not social realism,' Andrew Macdonald has stressed. 'It's a buddy movie. It's about a group of men, their friendship, loyalty and betrayal.' Yet this seems only half-right. If *Trainspotting* is a buddy movie, it is an oblique and corrupted one. Its inhabitants have more washed up together than forged proper friendships. Heroin anchors the tale and defines its characters. And looming above the other protagonists is Renton, who tries to come off the drug, back-slides, then finally succeeds. It is his trip towards redemption that the film follows, and yet, for all that, his eventual victory is never quite as life-affirming as it should be. For Renton has already been contaminated by a more legitimate but scarcely more savoury existence, hanging out amid the sharp-suited hyenas on the London property scene. After flogging four kilos of heroin to a bunch of big-time gangsters, Renton absconds with the loot, ripping off his mates (all except Spud, who is left with his cut) and marching off into the cold dawn of a new tomorrow. 'The truth is that I'm a bad person, but that's going to change,' he informs us. 'I'm moving on, going straight and choosing life. I'm going to be just like you.' It is the questionable merit of this ambition that *Trainspotting* reflects on throughout. Is 'just like us', the film asks, really such a great thing to be?

Technically, *Trainspotting* is a *tour de force*. Danny Boyle's direction is gritty and realistic in some parts and hallucinatory in others, brilliantly matching the up-and-down rhythms of the junkie's existence. Lively intelligence and a wry gallows humour permeate the film. Its characters are neither monsters nor pathetic case-studies. Their interests are the interests of the majority of Britain's twentysomethings. They discuss football and music and film. Yet all the while heroin paralyses them, colours everything around them. In a sense *Trainspotting* is less buddy movie, and more warped rites-of-passage story. Renton's coming of age is marked by his success in coming off heroin. But the ending is beautifully ambiguous. The impression it leaves is that the new, improved Renton has not so much redeemed himself as escaped. Which is not quite the same thing.

Central to *Trainspotting* is its presentation of drug use. Heroin is evil, it acknowledges, but it is also attractive. Accordingly the film's progress covers a wide spectrum of shades. At the start Boyle's picture is light, almost playful. The viewer is pulled into a pattern of identification with the characters, revelling in their misadventures and general rakes' progress through life. From here the tale turns darker by degrees, culminating in the black-as-pitch withdrawal section in Renton's bedroom and Tommy's AIDS-ridden decline, before lightening to a steely grey realism for the final scenes in London. In other words the film acknowledges heroin as pleasurable, fun even, before turning the tables. Although *Trainspotting* picks up Renton's story in mid-flow, the film's journey is essentially the junkie's journey: from euphoria to hell to a possible future without drugs. Danny Boyle insists that:

Our guiding aim was always to try to be honest about heroin. So yes, the beginning of *Trainspotting* is completely seductive. The dilemma was that we wanted to make an entertaining film about something that is potentially lethal, something that people may find unacceptable.

Andrew Macdonald crystallized the film's ethos: 'It's an undeniable truth that drugs are pleasurable. Yet that's the one thing that seems to have caused the most controversy. We all know that drugs are exciting. That's why people take them.'

Trainspotting neither demonizes nor martyrs its characters. Renton, Sick Boy, Spud *et al.* are not sad, sorry dupes at the mercy of evil drug-dealers, but bright, everyday youths who elect to take heroin rather than face up to the tedious alternative of dead-end jobs, marriage and mortgage. 'To me, *Trainspotting* is not about drugs,' says Robert Carlyle. 'It's about the society that puts people in that situation, the level of nihilism that means you'd rather lie smacked out in a corner than take part in life.' What *Trainspotting* does, then, is hook drug use into the widest possible framework, questioning why the youth of Britain take drugs and subtly showing that the alternative (Renton suited and booted and toiling away at an estate agents) is not really so great an improvement.

From the film's earliest days there came a rumbling concern over its stance on heroin addiction. Vague rumours filtered from the set of real-life drug use among the cast ('total bollocks' said Jonny Lee Miller). Later, in a location report for BBC's *Film 95*, Boyle mused whether the world had reached a stage when its inhabitants could engage in recreational drug use without fear of the consequences – speculation that earned a stiff rebuke from presenter Barry Norman. In truth, there looked to be a faintly spin-doctored quality to such events.

Certainly Boyle's comments, on so mainstream a programme as *Film 95*, appeared designed to provoke a reaction. Likewise, the prospect of clean-cut, middle-class actors 'going native' amid the smack-heads of Scotland did nothing to harm the film's street-cred. Miller, McGregor and Bremner denied such charges vehemently, yet it's a safe bet that the gossip had them tickled pink.

For those anticipating an unequivocal condemnation of heroin abuse, *Trainspotting* was to prove a scandalously irresponsible piece of work. 'People think it's all about misery and desperation and death and all that shite, which is not to be ignored,' comments Renton at the start of the tale. 'But what they forget is the pleasure of it. Otherwise we wouldn't do it.' Some critics, though, reacted to the very concept of a 'fun' film about heroin addiction, and one which neither demonized nor martyred its characters, with outrage, and they were blinded to a proper examination of the film's aims and ideals. On the eve of release, the film's issues were batted back and forth on BBC's *Newsnight*, while several British reviewers took a dim view of its content. *Evening Standard* critic Alexander Walker hated it. 'In style, structure and subversive imagination, it recalls Stanley Kubrick's *A Clockwork Orange*,' he wrote, before adding his disclaimer: 'Kubrick's film made one think. Boyle's film, overall a clever pastiche of the senior director's style, makes one puke.' The *Daily Mail*'s Chris Tookey, who would later spearhead the campaign to have David Cronenberg's *Crash* banned in the UK, was equally scathing: '*Trainspotting* pours scorn on conventional values and pokes fun at capitalism while subscribing to a much more vicious and depressingly consumerist ethos of its own. It is not a film I would care to have on my conscience.'

On the night of its release, Ewan McGregor cropped up on Channel 4's *TFI Friday* to be interviewed by Chris Evans. By now the drugs debate was in danger of reaching epidemic proportions. Yet Evans's first question was superbly weighted. 'Do you think', he asked McGregor, poker-faced, 'that watching this film will make kids want to take up . . .' a dramatic pause, '. . . acting?' McGregor, braced wearily to field yet another drugs question, was momentarily caught flat-footed. Then he started grinning. 'Yeah,' came the reply; hugely amused; conspicuously relieved. 'Yeah.'

By this stage, McGregor's defence of *Trainspotting* was well rehearsed. No, he didn't feel it glamorized heroin. Yes, he did feel it was a moral movie and yet, no, he didn't feel movies had to push a heavy moral message at every turn. *Trainspotting*, he said, 'is a reality that's extreme. That's what films are. Five people shooting up heroin is less extreme than blowing someone's face off with a gun.'

Otherwise, McGregor surprised journalists anticipating some ultra-hip icon of the permissive society. The actor had a hefty capacity for alcohol, smoked endless Marlboros ('I'm smoking for England today,' he quipped to one interviewer). Yet he drew the line where drugs were concerned. Heroin scared him. Cocaine troubled him. And he had never been much into the rave scene. A daisy-chain of journalists wondered aloud whether *Trainspotting*'s star supported the decriminalization of drugs. McGregor was unequivocal:

> No, I don't actually. If drugs were legalized all that would mean is the government making a shitload more money. Also, I think that in many cases soft drugs do lead on to harder stuff. I'm not saying that if you smoke one joint you're going to be shooting up with Class As the following week, and obviously social factors play their part. But yeah, I suspect that there is a ladder that you climb.

He had never, he insisted, become involved in drugs himself. 'I can't help thinking about what my parents would think,' he said. 'It would fucking destroy them.'

Boyle, too, became accustomed to defending his film against accusations that it painted the drug in a positive light, and propagated the image of 'heroin chic'. He argued that *Trainspotting* eventually shows how prolonged use of heroin will kill the addict. Renton's anguished withdrawal, and the fate of virginal user Tommy, he felt, should be enough to put anybody off. Robert Carlyle was equally bewildered by the fuss. 'I don't see how anybody could see *Trainspotting* and fancy taking smack,' he says. 'If they do, then fuck 'em. They're wankers. Begbie's disgusting. Renton's disgusting. They all are. There's nothing nice about these people.'

In the end, *Trainspotting* escaped rather lightly and there were no serious calls for it to be banned, or even trimmed down by the censors. The film even received the seal of approval from National Heritage Secretary Virginia Bottomley, who described it as 'a harrowing film that leaves you in no doubt as to the ravages of drug addiction'.

On a more aesthetic level, *Trainspotting* attracted criticism, even from within the industry. For while Neil Jordan compared it to the best of sixties youth cinema and felt it to be 'like a sixties Dick Lester movie – in the best sense of the word', Mike Leigh disliked it, and so did Ken Loach, who accused it of presenting a 'distorted view' of British life. 'It's aggressively young and Tarantino-esque,' said Loach, 'with a lot of violence and what the Americans call in that horrible phrase that I loathe: "in-your-face". That's not true of the way we live in Britain.' Incidentally, 'In Your Face' was the cover headline for *Empire* magazine's February 1996 feature on the film; showing, perhaps, that Yank parlance is as much alive in British film criticism as it is in film production.

For some, *Trainspotting*'s zesty panache seemed too self-consciously American for a film purporting to be about life in Britain today. Yet the vast majority welcomed Boyle's film with open arms. Its stylized sweep was regarded as taking the best traits of US cinema and applying them seamlessly to the inner-city scene at home. The sentiment was perhaps best expressed by *Empire*'s oft-quoted slogan: 'Hollywood come in, your time is up. *Trainspotting* is here and it's toe-curlingly good.' *The Face*, too, hailed it as 'tremendous, destined to have even more of a cultural impact in this country than *Pulp Fiction* . . . *Trainspotting*', it continued, 'is a revelation and a revolution. It is, in short, no *Shopping*.' In fact, this was a shrewd bit of revisionism on behalf of the magazine, which two years previously had trumpeted *Shopping* as 'the sexiest British movie of the year'. But no matter. *Trainspotting*, it was generally acknowledged, was the real McCoy. Here was a film that got the mix just right. It combined a darting, bracing, stylistically innovative mode of storytelling usually found in the American indies with an inner-city British landscape traditionally documented in stolid social-realist terms. *Trainspotting* was both surrealistic and naturalistic, fantastical and gritty, hip and harrowing. It trod a dangerous thematic tightrope and did so with a confidence and panache that took the breath away.

Inevitably, though, some viewers felt that the film's light and dark aspects made an uneasy marriage. 'There was a big premiere in Glasgow and it went down really well,' recalls Susan Vidler.

> But at the point where the baby died, a woman stood up and shouted, "You're all sick!" Apart from that, it was received really well. I should have realized it was going to be so popular because the stage play was incredibly successful: sold out every night. So there was obviously something about the stories that interested people, although a lot has to do with the way it was marketed. It was sold as a sexy film to go and see, and a sexy film to want to be able to talk about.

Trainspotting's official release date could hardly have been more significant. Only three first-run films went into UK distribution on Friday, 23 February 1996:

Trainspotting, *Sense and Sensibility* and *Casino*. In the landscape of British cinema, Ang Lee's *Sense and Sensibility* occupied the other end of the scale to Boyle's junkie saga. This proved a delicate adaptation of Jane Austen's period novel, starring Emma Thompson (who also wrote the screenplay) and rising-star Kate Winslet. In terms of content and aesthetics *Trainspotting* had more in common with *Casino*, Martin Scorsese's near-three-hour odyssey through the gambling scene of 1970s Las Vegas. Prior to filming, Boyle had had his cast sit through Scorsese's *GoodFellas* (as he had before making *Shallow Grave*), and *Casino* certainly stuck close to the *GoodFellas* format. It was broad and panoramic, its plotline only properly kicking in during the final hour. But where *GoodFellas* was fresh and vital, *Casino* occasionally showed signs of strain, and this was coupled with a general lack of ambition. While it was still a fine movie, Scorsese had made better ones, and now Boyle had too. In borrowing conspicuously from Scorsese's kinetic, visceral mode of film-making, the Manchester-born director had somehow conspired to beat the master at his own game.

Of course, not everyone felt this way. Writing in *Village Voice*, critic Amy Taubin took issue with various aspects of this strange British export, including its lead actor.

> McGregor's face is more glamorous than threatening, and so is the film – which wouldn't be a problem if it wasn't trying so hard to pass as subversive . . . What fails is Danny Boyle's direction. Boyle, who spent a decade in the theatre, is clearly no Scorsese. He's barely a director at all . . . He only has the crudest notion of how camera movement or placement can be expressive or make meaning.

In the States, too, the drugs debate continued to dog the film. In the summer of 1996, Republican presidential contender Bob Dole descended on the movie as part of a wider assault on what he saw as the evils of Hollywood (Hollywood, in this case, meaning any mainstream movie from around the globe). 'Yeah, and then he lost,' remarked McGregor wryly. 'So who cares what he thinks?'

Dole's intervention, though, was testament to the sheer broad-based impact of Boyle's film. After a succession of false starts and misguided follies, *Trainspotting* got the formula right. Here was a British film, with British concerns: modern, localized, idiosyncratic and without a big-star cast or an American actor to sweeten the pill for Stateside audiences. And yet, for all that, the finished product broke out of the art-house ghetto and found the widest possible audience.

The figures tell an impressive tale. On home soil, *Trainspotting* proved the most successful British-funded film of 1996, and did so by a long chalk. Its hefty domestic takings of £12,331,000 were nearly five times that of its nearest rival, Mark Herman's *Brassed Off* (also starring McGregor), which pulled in £2,873,000. Considering *Trainspotting*'s 18 certificate, which cut out a huge portion of its potential audience, this was an astonishing achievement. More crucially, *Trainspotting* created a bridgehead into the foreign markets, amassing a respectable $16.5 million in America (a territory where *Shallow Grave* had conspicuously failed to do business). By the year's end *Trainspotting*'s worldwide box-office returns had levelled out at $72 million. Compare this to the year's biggest hit, the crass sci-fi extravaganza *Independence Day*, which grossed $785 million, and *Trainspotting*'s success seems modest. But number crunch those figures again: judged solely on a budget-to-box-office ratio (a $3.5 million outlay for a $72 million return), *Trainspotting* finished up as 1996's most profitable picture.

Pinpointing the reasons for this success is tricky. It's tempting just to go with McGregor's own analysis that *Trainspotting* is simply 'a fucking great film:

no more, no less' and leave it at that. But inevitably, and frustratingly, there's more to it than that. At its most basic level, *Trainspotting* was already a proven commodity. Irvine Welsh's novel had already whipped up that crucial blend of controversy and critical acclaim in uncovering a slice of British life rarely before rendered as art. Moreover, the subsequent stage play, starring Bremner as Renton, had demonstrated that Welsh's tale could work equally well in another medium. So Boyle, Macdonald and Hodge's gamble was tempered by the knowledge that they were backed up by winning material with a proven pedigree.

In its execution, too, *Trainspotting* proved a mini-masterwork of style impacting on content. It side-stepped a worthy, hectoring interpretation of Welsh's saga in favour of a tempered approach which paradoxically managed to be both more subtle (by not pushing an anti-drugs message down the viewers' throats) and yet more cartoonish (filmed in the speedy, fast-cutting style of your average pop promo or youth-targeted TV commercial). In short, it caught the audience which such directors as Paul Anderson, Danny Cannon and Vadim Jean had tried and failed to snare. This crucial 18–25 demographic had hitherto rarely spent money to see a British movie. But *Trainspotting* spoke their language. It addressed their concerns, shared their humour and interests and, most importantly, did so in a seemingly authentic fashion. The controversy did it no harm either, and yet Boyle's brisk style lightened Welsh's original tone and kept the action and comedy coming quickly. *Trainspotting* managed to be dangerous, risky, edgy – and all without ever alienating its core audience.

Moreover, the film was packaged to perfection, aided no doubt by a hefty £800,00 production budget. *Trainspotting*'s release was preceded by a snazzy, custom-built trailer (as opposed to a simple taster sample of the film's content) and a distinctive ad campaign which introduced its lead characters in a sly pastiche of the old collectors'-cards system with each protagonist numbered and named by way of a semi-formal introduction. So influential was the orange *Trainspotting* poster that it was parodied almost instantly to promote the February 1996 re-release of Bruce Robinson's cult British comedy *Withnail and I.* Before too long the cheesy West End musical *Starlight Express*, desperately seeking a little of the movie's reflected glory, had followed suit in its own poster campaign.

Trainspotting also employed the tactic, perfected by Tarantino on *Reservoir Dogs* and *Pulp Fiction,* of underpinning its action with a telling pop soundtrack. The accompanying *Trainspotting* soundtrack was a classic, fittingly blending a crop of British and American music. Iggy Pop's 'Lust for Life' shifts into New Order's 'Temptation', through Blondie's 'Atomic' (re-done by Sleeper), Primal Scream's title track, Pulp's quirky 'Mile End', before Underworld's haunting 'Born Slippy' plays us into the closing credits. In the wake of the film's release Underworld (previously a culty dance act) found 'Born Slippy' ushered into the British top ten.

Meantime, Lou Reed's 'Perfect Day' (lilting in the background throughout Renton's nightmarish overdose) brought the former Velvet Underground frontman a whole new army of fans. Reed himself seemed quite bewildered by the attention. 'Everyone keeps talking about this *Trainspotting*,' he was to remark. 'What is it – an Australian film?' At the tail-end of 1997 the BBC ran a licence-fee commercial featuring an ensemble rendition of the song (the likes of Reed, David Bowie, Bono, Tom Jones and Boyzone each singing a line) and 'Perfect Day' went to number one. For the majority of *Trainspotting*'s viewers, Reed's song made an ironic, airy counterpoint to the horrors unfolding on screen. For the British record-buying public, it became the ultimate nostalgia-fest; the tender love song *par excellence*. In fact, the tune's pedigree was rather more shady. True, 'Perfect Day' was a love song, but not the kind most people took it for. Instead Reed offered a valentine to heroin; and the junkie hymn functioned as a kind of sly double-dialogue in Boyle's film.

However, Lou Reed wasn't the only one to benefit from the movie. *Trainspotting* had the Midas touch for practically all those associated with it. Success, by and large, bred success. Three months after the film came out, Kevin McKidd consolidated his position as one of Scotland's finest young actors with the release of Gillies and Billy MacKinnon's 1960s-set rites-of-passage drama *Small Faces*. Ewen Bremner has since interspersed TV work (*Harry Enfield and Chums*) with leading roles in *Mojo* (an adaptation of the Jez Butterworth stage play) and the rollicking, drug-fuelled outing *The Life of Stuff*. Peter Mullan, meanwhile, went from a minor support role as the drugs dealing Swanney to a lead turn in Ken Loach's *My Name is Joe*; a role which won him the Best Actor award at the 1998 Cannes Film Festival. Jonny Lee Miller, in particular, used *Trainspotting* as his career springboard. Since the film's release he has earned rave reviews for his turn as a shell-shocked squaddie in Gillies MacKinnon's First World War drama *Regeneration*, cropped up in Alan Rudolph's *Afterglow*, opposite an Oscar-nominated Julie Christie, and has been reunited with Robert Carlyle for the racy period yarn *Plunkett and Maclean*. On a more personal level, Miller also walked away from the shoot best buddies with co-star Ewan McGregor. The two young actors subsequently became regular fixtures out on the pub and party scene in central London.

After *Trainspotting*, Kelly Macdonald returned for a time to the McJob circuit, tending bar in a club in Glasgow. But she, too, has since proved that her chance-in-a-million break playing Diane was no fluke. In January 1998, she cropped up in the title role of Cokey Giedroyc's *Stella Does Tricks*, a starkly naturalistic tale of a Scottish schoolgirl prostitute on the streets of London. Macdonald had fallen into *Trainspotting* by accident, with scant hope of success. 'There were all these lovely girls with long locks, like models, at the audition,' she remembers. 'We also had to give photographs. I had mine done in a booth half an hour before I went. They were awful.' Even once she had the job, Macdonald had played a restricted second fiddle to the lads, occupying only a few short minutes of actual screen time. *Stella Does Tricks*, then, marked her real coming of age. She was the star, and the focus was on her throughout. Director Cokey Giedroyc and she 'discussed everything in the six or seven weeks before shooting. Danny [Boyle] knew exactly what he wanted and would stop you if you were doing something outside his preconceptions. He'd say "No! Not that!" Danny was fantastic, but with Cokey it was more equal.' From *Stella Does Tricks*, she moved on to work with director Mike Figgis (of *Leaving Las Vegas* fame) on *Death and the Loss of Sexual Innocence* and on American indie film-maker Gregg Araki's *Splendor*, in which she played 'a lesbian exchange-student sculptress with blue hair'.

At the time of *Trainspotting*'s release Robert Carlyle was away in the dusty hills of Nicaragua shooting Ken Loach's *Carla's Song*. He had imagined Boyle's film would be a small-scale, fringe hit and was dumbfounded, upon his return home, to realize how much of a splash it had made. 'I arrived back at Heathrow and Ewan's face was on every magazine,' he recalls. 'I thought it'd maybe be a cult film among people that knew the book.' For months afterwards, Carlyle became nervous of the monster he had created for himself in bringing Begbie to the screen – fretting about have-a-go thugs confusing art with reality and setting on him in the street. In the meantime, though, he continued to consolidate his position at the forefront of home-grown acting talent.

The shoot in Nicaragua was a gruelling experience, yet it paid big dividends. *Carla's Song* told the tale of a genial Glaswegian bus driver who gets caught up in the Sandinistas' struggle against the US-backed Contras and helped put a lot of distance between the actor and that troublesome Begbie image. Typically, Carlyle continued to immerse himself in research, too, coming away from Loach's film with an official bus driver's licence: 'Something I can fall back on if the acting work dries up.' In the year after *Trainspotting*, Carlyle also took the lead role in *Face*, an East End gangster fable from *Priest* director Antonia Bird, and – most famously – as the Sheffield doley marshalling a slovenly team of male strippers in Peter Cattaneo's *The Full Monty*. Although mainly bankrolled by American money, *The Full Monty* arguably eclipsed even *Trainspotting* in terms of public impact. By the close of 1997, it was being hailed as the most successful British film in history, outperforming even Mike Newell's American-tailored *Four Weddings and a Funeral*. As with most jackpot pictures, though, *The Full Monty* became caught up in controversy. At the forefront were rumbling threats of legal action from New Zealand playwrights Anthony McCarter and Stephen Sinclair, who claimed that scriptwriter Simon Beaufoy had lifted large portions of his tale from their 1987 stageplay *Ladies Night*. Meanwhile, in the background came rumours that the star and director had been split by creative differences throughout the shoot, with Carlyle ultimately taking on a lot of Cattaneo's directing duties. Perhaps it had been simpler playing a Glaswegian psychopath in a small, 'cult' production, after all.

Likewise poised to benefit from *Trainspotting* were its production team: Macdonald, Boyle and Hodge. And yet, paradoxically, the film's success put the triumvirate under immediate threat. Hodge, whose brilliant script job had laid the film's foundations, was Oscar-nominated in the category of Best Adapted

Screenplay, and travelled to the awards ceremony in Los Angeles, where he eventually lost out to Emma Thompson for *Sense and Sensibility*.

But Boyle and Macdonald were in LA too. Twentieth Century-Fox had offered the duo production and directing credits on *Alien Resurrection*, the fourth instalment in the ongoing sci-fi horror series. In movie-making terms this was the big league. Ridley Scott had directed the original *Alien*, James Cameron had directed the second chapter, *Aliens*, and David Fincher (who would later helm *Se7en*) the third. Had Macdonald and Boyle cashed in their chips after *Shallow Grave,* they would probably have been able to command a decent, mid-budget Hollywood outing. But *Alien Resurrection* was budgeted near the top of the Hollywood scale and promised to be an epic production, with Sigourney Weaver and Winona Ryder committed to star. Macdonald dreamed of keeping his unit together, and was already planning a new film based on an original script by Hodge. But *Alien Resurrection* was a powerful temptation. For a time it looked as though the Macdonald–Boyle–Hodge axis, with Ewan McGregor as their actor of choice, would not survive beyond two productions.

Calton Athletic suffered a more immediate crisis. After *Trainspotting*'s release, demand for their services skyrocketed. 'We have become', said founder David Bryce, 'a victim of our own success.' Calton made a reported £95,000 out of *Trainspotting*, but the money ran dry in the face of a barrage of new intakes, and in spring 1997 it looked as if the centre might have to close for good. Help came in the form of a charity football match that was played out on the sports-ground at Glasgow's Balleston Juniors Football Club on 11 June. The all-star team included McGregor, Carlyle, Miller, Irvine Welsh, Robbie Coltrane and Blur's Damon Albarn. Nearly a thousand spectators were in attendance (including Ewan's mum Carol) and over £40,000 was raised. Ewan scored two goals, perhaps giving lie to the earlier Calton claim over his lack of footballing skills, perhaps suggesting that the match was always more about putting on a show than serious competition. In the autumn a special-edition *Trainspotting* video, incorporating the original cinema trailer and a handful of previously unseen scenes, poured more money into the Calton coffers. With that, the centre's future was secured for at least another year.

In the meantime, Irvine Welsh, the father of the whole phenomenon, laboured to put his past behind him. He had initially written the book without much thought to it even being published and since watched from the sidelines as it took on a life of its own. Throughout it all, Welsh was determined to stay detached from the furore:

> *Trainspotting* has very little to do with me now. I can't take responsibility for the commercial appropriation and the hype. I have no power over it even if I had the will to change it.

He stays philosophical, though, likening the suddenly more dislocated, collaborative process to the evolution of house music:

> The original seventies artists have had their music sampled and you cannot be precious about it. The film and the play are just a remix of the book, and you have to see it that way. There's no point whingeing when you're making loads of money out of it.

Welsh moved on. In 1996, still sticking to the drugs milieu, the writer published *Ecstasy*, a loosely linked compendium of tales about the 'E' generation. But the book proved a pale shadow of his former triumph, and Welsh himself later expressed his dissatisfaction with it. *Trainspotting*, though, had entered the lexicon of the culture. It became a byword for hipness and decadence, and further galvanized the drugs debate in Britain.

Awkward and alluring, trendy and terrifying, sympathetic and condemnatory, *Trainspotting* is a Pandora's box of a film. As with all great movies it defies easy classification. Its myriad issues are all but impossible to map out clearly. In the event, it is perhaps too close to our culture, too 'in our face' to study from an objective perspective. And yet at the bottom line it is this precise quality which makes it so essential, so significant, such a mirror of our times. *Trainspotting* has become a film synonymous with nineties British culture, and its damned junkie characters, the closest thing the current cinema scene has to icons. Says Welsh:

> It does worry me that the characters have become heroes, because they should nae be held up as role models – they should be the reverse. But you have to accept that once a film is out, it is commonly owned. The way people respond to those things tells you about the kind of society we live in now.

At the crux of this epoch-catching film lay Ewan McGregor's Renton: a damned, desperate but wryly self-reflective emblem for our age. *Trainspotting* made McGregor a star. He took the lion's share of the publicity and his sodden, skinhead-cut pose became the film's abiding image. The picture signalled a time of change for the actor in both personal and professional terms. Immediately after filming finished, McGregor married girlfriend Eve Mavrakis in the grounds of a château in the Dordogne, 'with all my friends around and surrounded by sunflowers'. Then, in February of the following year, came the arrival both of *Trainspotting* and Ewan and Eve's daughter Clara Mathilde. The birth was complicated; twenty-four hours of labour culminating in a Caesarian section. At the end of it, McGregor staggered back to his Primrose Hill flat and stared disconsolately at the walls. 'I was out of my head,' he remembers.

'Suddenly it all became too much. I thought: "I'm young. I can't cope with all this." The weight of responsibility came down on me like a fucking ton of bricks.' After *Trainspotting*, events had a way of running out of McGregor's control.

BRANCHING OUT

6. BRANCHING OUT

Things speeded up after *Trainspotting*. The last four months of 1996 saw the arrival, in quick succession, of three more Ewan McGregor pictures: *The Pillow Book*, *Brassed Off* and an adaptation of Jane Austen's period merry-go-round *Emma*. It was a crazy blur of activity. He reflected:

> One minute I was lying on the floor with a syringe in my arm. Then I got married, then I was standing in this trailer with a top hat and leather gloves on, and for a moment I thought I can't go from skinhead drug addict to ha-ha-ha curly-wig acting.

But the actor was about to be judged on his adaptability and, in retrospect, the months after *Trainspotting* were critical for McGregor. Rather than fading from the scene, or becoming indelibly associated with one persona, the man was suddenly ubiquitous, cropping up in myriad guises. It marked his arrival as a truly multi-faceted British actor.

The leg work, though, had all been done the previous year. In 1995 McGregor went from a co-star role in Peter Greenaway's *The Pillow Book* to *Trainspotting* to *Emma* to *Brassed Off* with just a short break in the middle to marry Eve Mavrakis. Still more remarkable is the diverse range covered by this giddy quartet; ushering their star from art house to youth movie to high-gloss period romp to homespun political drama. Still relatively untried and inexperienced, McGregor adapted to each new terrain with the ease of an expert.

Of these four films McGregor made Peter Greenaway's *The Pillow Book* first. Thanks both to the general perversity of the film release schedule and the director's painstaking post-production process, it was the last of the four to appear at the cinema, finally being released nationwide in November 1996. Time telescoped once McGregor stepped off set. During the filming of *The Pillow Book*, he was just another young actor with a few films to his credit. When it was released he was arguably Britain's hottest movie star. 'He was a talented young kid and I treated him as such,' Greenaway reflects ruefully. 'Had I known what would become of him I might have shown a little more reverence.'

Regarded variously as iconoclastic and puritanical, and reviled and adored in about equal measure, Greenaway has never been an actors' director in the way that his TV- or theatre-raised contemporaries invariably are. Greenaway trained in fine art and made his first cerebral short films on a BFI budget. 'I am often accused of being an intellectual exhibitionist,' he admits. 'It is curious that any attempt to use material away from the orthodox should arouse such hostility. I like making films that speculate.' Certainly Greenaway's features are more concerned with raising questions than offering tidy answers. These are lofty, rarified projects; canvases dominated by ideas as opposed to plot and character. Positioned within the picture, his protagonists grow elusive and intangible. They become less flesh and blood creatures, and more living art exhibits, aesthetic pieces to be moved to and fro against an ornate, sometimes grotesque background.

Greenaway sits uncomfortably with the bulk of modern cinema, preferring instead to plough his own rigorous, individualist furrow. He disdains conventional narrative cinema as 'formulaic and fossilized', falling depressingly short of its full aesthetic potential. 'I still don't think we've found the great pantheon of cinema painters that you can put alongside Michelangelo and da Vinci,' he argues. 'There is no equivalent in the cinema experience.'

Greenaway's *The Draughtsman's Contract*, *Prospero's Books* and his acclaimed *The Cook, The Thief, His Wife and Her Lover* pioneered a new strain of cinema: moody, elliptical, piercingly intelligent. But Greenaway came a-cropper with his gruelling, dystopic medieval mystery play *The Baby of Macon*, in 1993. *The Baby of Macon* took scurrilous glee in uglifying the usual conventions of costume cinema, but it was a remorseless experiment, and even die-hard acolytes recoiled from its one-note bleakness. The film was gone from cinemas within a month, giving rise to speculation that Greenaway's peculiar star was on the wane.

In response, Greenaway looked to the east, taking as his touchstone the real-life tenth-century 'pillow book' of Sei Shonagon, a girl courtier in the Japanese Heian Dynasty court. Sei's book amounted to 'a list of elegant things', and inspires modern girl Nagiko (Vivian Wu) to keep her own ('Just like her I could fill it with an account of my loves'). She hunts lovers with a skill at calligraphy and eventually encounters Jerome (McGregor), a British translator living in Kyoto. Jerome becomes 'a living sacrifice' for Nagiko, who decorates his body then delivers him to the publisher who has turned down her work. But when the arrangement turns sour, Jerome cracks up then kills himself. He ends up as a pillow book himself, his skin beaten into the pages of the publisher's manuscript.

The Pillow Book is a teasing, tantalizing puzzle of a film. In essence, it functions as a cool essay on how relationships operate in a landscape of intense semiotics and signifiers. The director lingers lovingly over the mechanics of calligraphy. 'The word for rain should fall like rain,' we are told. 'The word for smoke should drift like smoke.' When Greenaway puts a French love song on the soundtrack, he scrolls the lyrics across the screen, but does so in their native language. Nagiko's voice-over wraps itself around certain words, tenderly enunciating them. Words – their shape, their sound – are constantly fetishized.

McGregor was drawn to *The Pillow Book* after casting an eye over Greenaway's script. It was like no other screenplay he'd ever seen: a montage of drawings, doodles and long, ornate descriptions ('detail right down to the bone,' says Ewan). There was also a startling lack of scripted dialogue. This, it turned out, was for him to uncover himself, upon navigating each scene.

Generally judged to be Greenaway's most user-friendly film, *The Pillow Book* paradoxically provided Ewan McGregor with his most abstract and unclassifiable role to date. The actor trips through the piece as a kind of decorative conduit.

> This has been a very different experience for me, but I found it very stimulating. I regularly spent about two to four hours every day having calligraphy applied all over my body; very sensual and something I will not forget in a hurry.

The job of this fell to Japanese calligrapher Yukki Yaura, who adorned Ewan's body with a range of body paints. Accustomed to working on inanimate materials, Yuara lamented that the job was 'very difficult, because the paint was not fluid and dried very quickly'.

McGregor had hurdles to overcome too. He admits to finding the Greenaway method baffling. 'I don't know what it'll turn out like,' he fretted while the film was still in its post-production stage. 'I really had very little grip on what I was doing. I just wandered about and spoke occasionally. Very fucking strange.' The director's way with his actors was about as hands-off as it comes. As McGregor explained to *Time Out* magazine:

> Greenaway really is an artist. It sounds wanky, but it's true – he paints with the camera. They light it, then he'll go and adjust things around the set as if he's going to paint them. You're as important as the leaves on the tree in the background. He'd tell you come in here and you end up here and the rest is up to you!

More than perhaps any other director's film, Greenaway's movies come together during the editing stage. *The Pillow Book* is a veritable treasure-chest of digital conjury. There are frames within frames within frames. There are inserts and subtitles and overlays. The cinema screen becomes broken up and partitioned. It nudges the viewer through a series of different perspectives, which add up to a whole new process by which we, the audience, see or 'read' a film. This, of course, is Greenaway's aim. His Utopian vision for the future of cinema is for a more interactive, all-encompassing medium. The ideal state, he argues, is for the time-frame to be in the hands of the viewer and not the maker; where the empowered viewer can spend as long as desired on any portion of the film, like lingering in front of a favourite painting in an art gallery. *Guardian* writer Jonathan Romney offers an illuminating elaboration when he compares *The Pillow Book* to a CD-rom, 'or one of those limited edition art books printed on paper so delicate you need to wear linen gloves to turn the pages'.

In the minds of critics and public alike, *The Pillow Book* was seen as making amends for *The Baby of Macon*. Its warmer, more inclusive tone was reflected in a healthy showing at the box-office (aided, no doubt, by Ewan McGregor's post-*Trainspotting* stardom). But this was still a Greenaway film and, inevitably, it had its detractors. J. Hoberman, writing in *Village Voice*, took a tough line on the film:

> The riskiest thing about this soporific experiment is placing the word "pillow" in the title. It might give the viewer ideas . . . It is a staggering bore – as vacantly petulant as Kate Moss's stare.

This, though, is overly harsh. True, *The Pillow Book* is a narcissistic creature, but it is also worthwhile and intelligent: tastefully carnal and genuinely strange. Away from its languid discourse on semiotics, the film also did McGregor's status the power of good. Greenaway's mind may have been on higher things, but his film, perhaps inadvertently, provided a prolonged and impressive showcase for its lead actor's penis. 'The old chap' (McGregor's description) had already made a brief cameo in *Trainspotting* and on-stage during his days in the theatre ('The old dears in the audience would shriek and cover their eyes,' he remembers). But it came into its own during *The Pillow Book*. When the actor was at the 1996 Cannes Film Festival, Barry Norman took him aside and told him: 'I saw *The Pillow Book*. I see you dress to the right.'

The situation was a source of great amusement to McGregor. He told *Neon* magazine:

> The funniest thing about films like *The Pillow Book* is that people come up to me – and there's two schools on this one. There's the school that discusses the film's artistic content at great length. And there's other people that come up and

just, straight out, say: "I saw your cock on screen. I saw your penis four-foot long on a big piece of canvas".

McGregor's parents managed to embrace both schools of thought. After the film's release a letter from the folks spooled from his fax machine. 'They said [*The Pillow Book*] was one of the most beautiful things they had ever seen.' But at the end of the message his dad added a wry 'P.S: I am glad to see you have inherited one of my major attributes.'

The McGregor member was nowhere on show during *Emma*, and perhaps that was part of the problem. If McGregor was initially fretful over his work on *Trainspotting* and *The Pillow Book*, here he was openly dismissive. Even today, he rates *Emma* as his worst feature film, and one of his most bungled jobs as an actor. 'I can't even watch myself in that one,' he says, wincing. 'I look like a total fucking arsehole.'

The second Jane Austen adaptation of 1996 (after Ang Lee's *Sense and Sensibility*), *Emma* takes a broad-based, cleaned-up approach to one of the writer's most purely personal novels. *Emma* was originally written in 1815 as a playful experiment, an attempt by the author to create a central character 'who no one will like except myself'. Accordingly, Austen's Emma Woodhouse is bored, spoilt and meddlesome, beguiled by her singularly self-attributed skills as a matchmaker and moving the hapless citizens of her small Surrey township around like pieces on a chessboard. She is snobbish, casually callous and frustratingly blind to the call of her own heart. Yet, for all that, Emma emerges from the pages as a vital, endearing and oddly contemporary heroine. The reader roots for her, despairs for her and – against their better judgement at times – wills her on towards a happy ending.

Doug McGrath's version, though, blunts Austen's stiletto-witted observations. The whole affair views like some cartoon treatment rustled up by a GCSE student of Eng Lit. It is vibrant and lively, but its peppy, primary-coloured style tends to work against the intricacies of the text. Characters communicate through reams of dialogue interspersed with long, meaningful looks. Clues that were cleverly scattered and veiled in the book now scream out to be noticed. 'Actually I thought it was a pretty good adaptation of a very dull writer,' McGregor argues of the film as a whole. 'I don't like Jane Austen at all. I don't known why I did it, really.'

Emma was, from the off, a transatlantic affair. American McGrath cut his teeth as a journalist before moving into the film industry. In 1994 he helped Woody Allen co-write the script for his polished backstage farce *Bullets over Broadway*. But for his own writing–directing debut, McGrath looked back to an earlier inspiration. 'There's such a dearth of good material,' he said to explain his reasons for choosing Austen. 'So I think people come to her with renewed delight.'

The lead role, too, went to an American. At the time of shooting, twenty-one-year-old Gwyneth Paltrow, the daughter of an established Hollywood showbusiness couple, was best known for her head-in-a-box role in David Fincher's serial-killer shocker *Se7en*, and as the steady girlfriend of the film's star, Brad Pitt. Diligently wrestling with an English accent, Paltrow makes a decent fist of a demanding role. Surrounding her are a host of genuinely home-grown actors: Greta Scacchi as her governess, Polly Walker as her hapless rival and thirty-four-year-old Jeremy Northam, a shade too young and aquiline to convince as the distinguished Mr Knightley.

McGregor was allocated what amounts to a second-string role as Frank

Churchill, the dashing tearaway whom *Emma*, for a time, fancies she may be in love with. From the start, he cuts a faintly ridiculous figure, forced into breeches and a top hat under which spills a cascade of Farrah Fawcett-ish blond hair. McGregor stands at a piano, sings a hey-nonny-nonny-type song and generally looks pretty uncomfortable with his lot in life. 'The wig has a lot to do with it,' he admits. 'Also the accent; we were forced into doing this very clipped, proper English accent, so as a result I wasn't really talking to anyone. I was just trying to sound right.'

In its lightweight, breezy way Doug McGrath's *Emma* is satisfying enough. But it remains a mediocre picture, and arguably the least interesting project McGregor has yet been associated with. *Emma* is British heritage cinema via the Hollywood production line: over-designed, deodorized and rampantly fussy (frilly foliage has an irksome tendency to intrude into every scene). Reviews, too, were tepid. 'For a moment I thought Ewan McGregor as Frank Churchill, coming upon *Emma* stuck in the river with her horse and trap, was going to harden up the proceedings with an injection of a little iron,' wrote Derek Malcolm. 'But it comes to nothing, as does his part in the end.' McGregor's most scathing critic, though, was McGregor himself:

> I was so crap. I was terrible in it. I didn't believe a word I said. I just thought "Shut the fuck up, Frank." It was the first time for me: I was really embarrassed about it, and I'm not paranoid about that usually. But this time I didn't know what I was doing.

McGregor shies away from criticizing the film as a whole, but his comments hint at a wider insecurity running top to toe through McGrath's picture. *Emma* rolled before the cameras throughout the summer of 1995, its action set amid the green fields of rural Dorset. For though Austen had set her tale in Surrey, the

Home Counties had become too tamed and over-developed over the intervening 180 years. The West Country provided a more primitive-looking backdrop, with thick hedgerows dividing up a quiltwork of tiny fields. But if the setting was idyllic, the atmosphere certainly struggled to match it. Crew members recall it as a tense shoot with little in the way of camaraderie among the cast. According to on-set sources, Paltrow was kept cosseted and out of sight: the pampered queen of the castle. Below her a rigid film-making hierarchy soon developed.

For three days, the cast and crew took over the picturesque village of Evershot (doubling as Austen's Highbury). The experience degenerated into near farce, as Middle England collided with the moneyed movie world. Miramax (the film's backers) paid £3,000 for the three days of shooting. In response, Dorset County Council agreed to shut down Fore Street – Evershot's central artery of thatched cottages with abundant window boxes – and impose trespass fines of £400. Locals were shooed off set, and cameras, cables, lighting rigs and trailers came to dominate the town. The lads of the area, hiding in the margins to catch a glimpse of rising starlet Paltrow, were unimpressed. One reckoned her to be 'thin and pasty-faced'. Another scoffed at the way the actress was treated: 'When she fell over and cut her knee there were twelve people to catch her before she hit the ground.'

Policing the front line was Evershot man Matt Potter, whom Miramax paid £50 a day to serve as an unofficial community liaison officer. Potter's job put him in the role of a little Hitler: blocking off roads, desperately hushing talkative locals or nearby car engines. 'I'm in the worst position, really,' he lamented. 'The village people want me to get the film crew to do things for them and the film people want me to calm down the village. I'll be glad when it's finished.' Potter's worst moment on the job came when an irate motorist approached him brandishing a baseball bat. On the ground level, *Emma* offered conclusive proof that Hollywood and everyday England make uneasy bedfellows.

If McGregor felt the *Emma* shoot to be fraught, *Brassed Off* was even worse. Irate locals in deepest Dorset are still locals from deepest Dorset: generally affluent, middle class and passive. Irate locals in the depressed mining town of Grimethorpe are something else entirely. There were moments when the cast and crew of Mark Herman's pit-closure drama felt as though they were picking their way through a war zone.

Writer–director Herman had wanted to spotlight the mining dispute since 1992, when the then President of the Board of Trade Michael Heseltine's accelerated programme of pit closures had galvanized public opinion, culminating in a well-supported protest march through the leafy streets of west London. That same year, Herman had been doing the rounds with his *Blame it on the Bellboy*, a threadbare, frivolous farce which met with poor audiences and reviews that verged on the contemptuous. Herman (who has never disowned *Blame it on the Bellboy*) hungered to tackle something more serious. A Yorkshireman, Herman had sold bacon for his family firm in Hull before training as an animator. The Tory government's treatment of Britain's mining industry enraged him, and he felt the other side of the story needed telling. 'I wanted to write something about pit closures,' he said. 'But they're not very cinematic. I needed something to hang it on.'

The hook came when Herman spotted a news story about the Grimethorpe Colliery brass band, who had won a competition at the Royal Albert Hall just days after the town's mine was closed by British Coal. In truth, Grimethorpe Colliery Band were professional musicians, not miners, and after the colliery shut were given what band-leader Frank Renton called 'a very good golden handshake' from British Coal. But Herman saw in the news item the makings of a powerful drama: lives and livelihood ripped apart; artistic expression made obsolete; an age-old tradition confined to the dustbin with no thought to the human consequences. The brass-band angle anchored *Brassed Off*, shrewdly merging the political with the personal.

Film Four agreed to back Herman's film on the strength of a one-page synopsis. With the script completed, Miramax stepped in and doubled its budget. Casting went just as smoothly. The soulful, raw-boned Pete Postlethwaite came on board to play Danny, the ailing, never-say-die band leader. Stephen Tompkinson (previously best known as the skittish reporter on Channel 4's *Drop the Dead Donkey*) would play his son, Ewan McGregor the young pup French-horn player and Tara Fitzgerald the flugelhorn temptress who's secretly in thrall to the Coal Board bosses.

Shooting was scheduled for the autumn of 1995 in locations around Halifax and Doncaster. Grimethorpe, though, was the principle base, doubling as the thinly disguised alter ego of Grimley. Grimethorpe Colliery had closed two years before. Margate Street and Brighton Road were awash with boarded-up shops and derelict homes. Unemployment was nosing 50 per cent and pregnancy rates among thirteen- to twenty-five-year-olds had rocketed. There was no industry, no cohesion and little optimism for the future. One local councillor likened the town to Northern Ireland.

With the townsfolk suspicious of rich movie moguls overrunning them, this was a landscape to be trod through warily. Herman wisely imposed a strict ban on limousines, driving on to set himself in a battered old hatchback. But when various items of equipment went missing, security was tightened, prompting threats of firebomb attacks against the crew. 'We naively expected the police to defend us, but there's only one policeman there,' recalls Herman. 'He's about forty but he looks eighty. And he told me: "They know where I live."'

Tara Fitzgerald had been raised in comparative comfort in the Caribbean and Richmond before sliding smoothly into London's acting scene. She describes herself as 'a champagne socialist: very unpoliticized', and grim up-North Grimethorpe came as a shock. Initially Fitzgerald dubbed the place 'the shit-hole of nowhere'. Later she took a more diplomatic tack:

> I've never been in a town with its heart just ripped out like that, its spirit just crushed . . . When we first arrived people were very suspicious of us. There was a lot of threatening behaviour. You had to bolt everything down on set or it would go walking. [Grimethorpe] made me feel I come from another, soft part of the world.

With *Emma*, the lines had been clearly drawn and rigorously policed. Here, cast and crew soon decided to opt for a proactive approach, mixing with the locals and shooting pool at the working-men's club. Herman noticed a marked improvement:

> Once people had grasped the fact that we were there to film a very valid and honest story and not to exploit them in any way, the co-operation was outstanding and very gratifying. I think the local people realized we were very much on their side.

From this point on the behaviour and dry gallows humour of the Grimethorpe inhabitants seems to have become more intriguing than frightening. While shooting one street scene, Tara Fitzgerald noticed a young girl playing recklessly in the road. The actress called over the girl's brother and told him he had better rescue her before she got hurt. 'She better not get herself killed,' the boy said, frowning. 'We could never afford a coffin.' On another occasion Tompkinson stood to one side while an ancient ex-miner shaped up for a long pot at the pool table. 'He'll never make that,' a regular whispered in his ear. 'He doesn't go that far on his holidays.' Late afternoon on Guy Fawkes Day, Herman ran across two kids on their way into the town centre. He asked them what they were up to that night. 'We're going to go and burn down the Co-op,' they told him. 'Naturally I assumed they were joking,' says the director. 'But when we turned up the next day it was gone.'

Coarse-grained socialist Postlethwaite took it more in his stride.

There may well be more exotic locations than the south of Yorkshire in late autumn, but there's nowhere else that touches it for friendliness and warm-heartedness. I can't think of many other films where the atmosphere was so positive and warm.

In the end, then, the *Brassed Off* army left Grimethorpe on much better terms than they had arrived. Postlethwaite kept his conductor's baton as a souvenir. To this day Fitzgerald keeps her honorary membership card to Grimethorpe Working Men's Club tucked away in her purse.

Brassed Off opens with a constellation of lights in the gloom: a band of miners picking their way out of the pit. It goes on to become a strangely old-fashioned picture, a straight-down-the-line yarn with its heart on its sleeve; an affectionate salute to the working-man's spirit; a righteous condemnation of Tory government policy. Herman's film has its problems. In its worst moments its humour seems antiquated and *Carry On*-esque – all flirty innuendo and away-day coach trips. Yet *Brassed Off* ultimately makes its picture-postcard style work in its favour. In the second half it subtly darkens in tone before blossoming in its final moments to become a heart-wrenching farewell to an entire way of British life. *Brassed Off* is sentimental (the band members sing 'Danny Boy' outside the dying Postlethwaite's hospital window) and emotionally manipulative (the crashing climactic rendition of the '1812 Overture'). Yet, for all that, its moral force is impossible to ignore. Frank Renton, the original Grimethorpe conductor, took issue with the film's final scene where Postlethwaite rails at the government from the Royal Albert Hall stage. 'This foul-mouthed political speech from the rostrum was just a bit cheap and nasty to me,' he sniffed, 'And I don't think it will elevate the image of brass bands in anybody's mind.' *Brassed Off* proved him wrong. Sales of brass-band music soared after the film's release.

If Herman's aim was to raise the profile of Britain's unemployed miners, he succeeded spectacularly. In the House of Commons, Labour backbencher Dennis Skinner fired a question at Virginia Bottomley, the Secretary of State for National Heritage:

> Doesn't the Secretary of State agree that one of the best British films of the past few months is *Brassed Off*? It is about a mining community where the pit has shut and the community has been destroyed as a result of the Tory government, and where the pit band is trying to find enough money to continue playing.

Bottomley, though, managed to sidestep the central point. She was pleased to be able to say that many brass bands throughout Britain were now receiving funds from the National Lottery, etc, etc.

As with *Emma*, Ewan McGregor plays more of a background role in *Brassed Off*. But here he proves much more adept. The lion's share of the glory gets split between Postlethwaite – who gives a rigid, desperate, achingly effective performance – and Tompkinson, who brings a wounded anguish to his role as the tears-of-a-clown coal worker forced to earn his keep as an entertainer at children's parties. Fitzgerald and McGregor, meantime, play the everyday, comparatively uncomplicated young lovers. Shaggy-haired and rumpled,

McGregor breezes through the part with the ease of an expert. The role marked him out, said the *Village Voice*'s Amy Taubin, as 'that rare thing, an unabashedly romantic actor'.

Trainspotting, Emma, Brassed Off and *The Pillow Book*: each utterly distinct, each tilting a different side of McGregor to the light; showcasing a different aspect of his flourishing expertise. All made in 1995, all released the following year. Ewan McGregor's year of arrival was 1996. Throughout it all he continued working, moving from role to role, movie set to movie set, with neither the time nor the inclination to sit back and enjoy the limelight. 'I knew it was happening and yet I didn't know, if you see what I mean. I was too busy working.' In the meantime – and apparent to everybody bar himself – McGregor had become a star.

McGREGOR THE ACTOR

7. McGREGOR THE ACTOR

Good acting relies on illusion. If you're aware of a performance unfolding, the chances are that it's bad acting. 'The art of acting is not to act,' explains Anthony Hopkins. 'Once you show them more, what you are showing them, in fact, is bad acting.'

Ewan McGregor's skill as a performer – his budding genius, even – is that you are rarely aware of the performance. On screen the magic looks effortless. You can't see the wires: there is no sweat and no perceivable effort which threatens to snap you out of the spell. McGregor moves from picture to picture, transforming himself to fit flushly into the tone and content of each new story. He becomes, in the best sense of the term, a part of the film's furniture.

And yet, inevitably perhaps, it is not quite as simple as that. For McGregor's star status rests on an image, on a widespread-recognition factor. He is not a career chameleon like Robert De Niro or Daniel Day-Lewis – actors who pride themselves on expunging any trace of personality, on dashing preconceptions, on vanishing without trace into the guts of each new project. McGregor is not as rigorous a craftsman, and nor presumably does he want to be. Take the finest McGregor creations: Renton in *Trainspotting*, Jerome in *The Pillow Book*, Robert the bungling kidnapper in *A Life Less Ordinary*. Each character is clearly defined; each vastly different from the other but always perfectly in tune with the tone of the picture he inhabits. Yet each is still, at some level, indelibly, ineffably Ewan McGregor. The spine of the man's personality remains, whatever costume you drape across it. Compared with De Niro or Day-Lewis, his acting style is a kind of halfway submergence. Like the Cheshire Cat, a wry and knowing grin hangs in the air as the rest of him sinks into his work, a tell-tale acknowledgement of the man behind the role. As *Time Out* critic Tom Charity puts it: 'You watch him for who he is, not for who he's pretending to be.'

It is this quality that sets McGregor aside from most of his British contemporaries, and from the underlying trend in cinema acting in general. It is a style which has also hastened his arrival as a bona fide British film star – at a time when most actors are still rattling around on the fringes of the medium. Whatever the role, and whatever the film – regardless of his performance – McGregor is always, on some level, McGregor: a reassuring point of reference for the ticket-buying public.

The clues to the McGregor mode of working lie in his childhood; slouched in the living room of his parents' home in Crieff in front of a procession of black-and-white classics from the Hollywood Golden Age. 'Anything black and white with strings down the picture, anything soppy and sentimental,' he remembers. 'I was well into it.' The youthful McGregor was not short of role models. His uncle, Denis Lawson, provided a contemporary touchstone, a flesh-and-blood success story from his own family. But for his real filmic influences, McGregor cast further back. Cary Grant was a hero, as were Gary Cooper and Henry Fonda. Towering above them all, though, went the homespun figure of James Stewart.

Born in Pennsylvania and educated at the prestigious Princeton University, Stewart quickly evolved into one of Hollywood's most successful actors in the 1930s. Immigrant director Frank Capra plucked him from the ranks of other jobbing actors and both identified and expanded on the crucial characteristics of his on-screen image. Tall (six-foot-three) and gangly, Stewart came to embody a peculiarly American brand of decency. He was the young, awkward everyman: slow of speech but honest as the day; a shade unglamorous (particularly when compared to rival actors like Cary Grant or Clark Gable) but strong where it counted. Quietly, efficiently heroic. A trio of Capra classics effectively defined the Stewart image. He played the soulful, rebellious rich-kid in 1938's *You Can't Take it with You*, the straight-arrow small-town politician battling the powers-that-be in the following year's *Mr Smith Goes to Washington*, and a small-town saint in 1946's immortal *It's a Wonderful Life* (the actor's own favourite from among his films). Around this trio were scattered a whole host of other Hollywood films which vigorously exploited the Stewart style, among them *The Shop around The Corner* (as an earnest young sales clerk), *Harvey* (as a benign town drunk) and *The Philadelphia Story* (as an outwardly cynical, inwardly sweet tabloid reporter).

Stewart, though, was no contrived or sugary performer. Even in his most sentimental roles, there was an impact to his acting, an easy grace which carried him over the sticky patches. After the Second World War, he deliberately added some blacker hues to his palette, allowed his familiar persona to be warped and revised. John Ford cast him as a phony hero in his subtle, revisionist Western, *The Man Who Shot Liberty Valance*, while Alfred Hitchcock placed the actor in three roles that would radically overhaul his image. In *Rope* Stewart played a cold, Nietzschean philosopher, in *Rear Window* a compulsive voyeur and in *Vertigo* a potential necrophile. Such roles complicated the Stewart myth. Some critics singled him out as the quintessential American actor, whose career progress in some ways mirrored that of the nation as a whole. Before the Second World War, Stewart was simple, soulful, young and idealistic. After it he grew darker, more cynical, more ambiguous, reflecting America's own slide into the Cold War.

As a child, McGregor's favourite Stewart films were *It's a Wonderful Life* and *Harvey*, two good-natured yet intelligent and, at times, deceptively ambiguous dramas. Each film provided an ideal showcase for the repertoire of its star. Perhaps McGregor was initially hooked by the familiar name (Stewart is dad James's middle name). Perhaps he identified with the Stewart image. Whatever the reasons, Stewart became the actor he most admired, the one he most sought to emulate.

These influences hook McGregor into an altogether older tradition of movie acting. Actors like Stewart, Grant and Fonda cut their teeth in vaudeville, or in the theatre. Their subsequent success was dependent on whether an audience would find them winning or charismatic. At the time of their break into movies, Hollywood was governed by the star system. Actors were contracted to their respective studios. They perfected a persona and stuck to it; riffing off it at times and varying the tone, but rarely breaking from it entirely. They were packaged commodities; selling a lifestyle, an image which they held the patent on. They were actors by craft; movie stars by reputation.

● ● ● ● ●

The landscape began to change in the 1950s. The Method approach, spearheaded by younger men like Marlon Brando, Montgomery Clift and James Dean, broke from the past to put more emphasis on the performance and less on the persona. Of course, in their own ways, Brando, Clift and Dean were peddling an image too: the wild man, the lost soul, the rebel teenager. Where it differed was that the Method performers were not trying to win over their audience, to charm them with charisma, grace or perfectly delivered lines. Inspired by the naturalistic acting style first developed by Stanislavsky in the nineteenth century, the Method became a powerful artistic mode; first in the theatres of New York, later in the moneyed, conservative world of Hollywood. The aim, said Method actor Eli Wallach, was 'a rebellion against posturing, singing orators, technically polished and emotionally empty actors'. This new breed aimed to shake the audience, to make them uncomfortable, even to leave them alienated. Their characters were tortured, untrustworthy, volatile anti-heroes. By this time Stewart was experimenting with more ambiguous roles himself, in *Vertigo* and *The Man Who Shot Liberty Valance*, but he hailed from a different time and a different tradition. He could never hope to capture the untreated energy or turbulent style of the new bloods on the block. Compare him to Brando in *A Streetcar Named Desire*, Dean in *Rebel without a Cause*, or Clift in *From Here to Eternity* and the contrast in styles is striking.

For most actors who've learned their craft during the last thirty years, the Method technique has become their lynchpin. They might reject the Method as a means of training, but the impact of its most famous exponents is hard to shake off. Brando and Dean, in particular, acquired celebrity status as anti-heroes. They were uncompromising, individualistic and spoke directly to a new generation of movie-goers. When the next generation of American actors broke through (Jack Nicholson, Robert De Niro, Harvey Keitel), the legacy of their predecessors coloured and conditioned their own performances. The easy charm of Stewart, Grant and Fonda, while still regarded with affection, and even reverence, has nonetheless dwindled as an influence.

In Britain, the Brando–Clift–Dean axis had a similar influence. The sixties saw the rise of the Free Cinema movement in British film. Working-class actors like Albert Finney (*Saturday Night and Sunday Morning*), Tom Courtenay (*The Loneliness of the Long Distance Runner*) and Richard Harris (*This Sporting Life*) seized the opportunity to show a side of British masculinity rarely before explored on film. Today, the influence of these groundbreaking pictures still resonates. The best of current British talent – Robert Carlyle, Ian Hart, Christopher Eccleston, David Thewlis, Tim Roth – acknowledge the Free Cinema/kitchen-sink school as a major influence on their own work. Clearly they hail from different disciplines than the likes of Kenneth Branagh and Ralph Fiennes, actors reared on the more traditional, purely British pedigree of Shakespeare and stage work.

McGregor, though, doesn't fit in with either school. For a man at the centre of what is quite possibly the decade's most contemporary picture, his pedigree looks determinedly old school. In contrast to the majority of his fellow British actors, he rejects the obvious influences of De Niro, Brando and Nicholson.

> It's not that I don't like them, but I find it very difficult to have someone who's still making movies as a hero in acting, because people are brilliant in some parts and not brilliant in others. Those people have made an awful lot of crap along with the good stuff. You look at the old-school Hollywood greats and their body of work is just much more.

On *Trainspotting*'s release, the film was frequently compared to Kubrick's amoral, incendiary *A Clockwork Orange*. At the time, Ewan provoked surprise, and not a little disbelief, by claiming that he had never seen the picture and had never even heard of its star, early 1970s Brit icon Malcolm McDowell. Blissfully unaware of much of recent cinema, his inspiration hails from an antique time; in those heady days before the arrival of Technicolor, when nihilism wasn't trendy and the Method hadn't been fully assimilated within mainstream film production. Even today, McGregor appears unashamedly nonplussed by this fundamental film theory. 'The Method,' he says. 'I've never been entirely sure what that means, actually.'

McGregor reckons he would have fitted very nicely into the glamorous world of 1940s Hollywood.

> I know I have a terrible tendency to romanticize that time in Hollywood which was probably just as full of shit as it is now, but I like not to think so. The idea of being attached to a studio and doing four movies for them a year is very appealing to me. They dressed amazingly, rode about in big cars and went to fantastic parties. People were really movie stars back then.

In this way, McGregor stands out as a peculiarly postmodern creature: a modern British film star inspired by a forgotten time and a defunct system in a foreign land, unconsciously aping the bearing of the Hollywood greats. Like Stewart, Fonda or Grant, he is an animal of ready grace and boundless charisma. Like them, he looks natural and at ease before the camera. Yet McGregor's acting style is no karaoke retread of the past. He takes his old-school influences and marries them seamlessly to a modern-day milieu: age and youth, old and new bound together in an easy, harmonious fusion.

Of course, such ease is the result of enormous technical expertise. The natural 'look' comes at a cost. McGregor's training at Perth, Kirkcaldy and Guildhall, and later on-the-job experience in a variety of roles, and for a variety of directors, has no doubt equipped him with a powerful arsenal of acting skills. Yet one suspects that McGregor possesses an instinctive feel for performing that he has probably never been entirely without. Significantly, he felt restricted and limited when forced towards more formal training at Guildhall, and became self-conscious and awkward about his ability. 'It took me two years to get rid of that feeling,' he claims. 'To get back to where I had been.'

As opposed to actors like De Niro, Ian Hart, Day-Lewis, or even Robert Carlyle, who revel in the nuts and bolts of the acting craft, McGregor approaches it in a more intuitive fashion. There is a sense that acting for him is a giddy game, an extension of the rampages he went on as a kid in the hills behind Crieff. He is wary of taking it too seriously, of rationalizing his craft, or of talking it to death. 'I just love acting,' he says with a shrug. 'It's a great thing to do.' Danny Boyle agrees: 'One good thing about him is that he doesn't waste time intellectualizing the work. He deals with everything very immediately.' All of which makes McGregor, in some respects, the last of the great British amateurs: the naive, native genius, with an easy and unhurried air, in a world of stern professionals.

Such instinctive gifts give McGregor a self-confidence rare in the acting world. He is secure enough in his skills that he feels no need to dominate, to hog the screen, or upstage his co-stars. Even in brief cameos, actors like Brando (*A Dry White Season*), De Niro (*Angel Heart*) or Nicholson (*Broadcast News*) tend to dwarf the rest of action. Their presence is so charged that they spill out from the frame and all too often destabilize the picture as a whole. McGregor, on the other hand, is content to remain in the background and let others seize the glory, if the part calls for it. In other words, he sustains a brilliant balance throughout his work. He is always, on some level, Ewan McGregor, and yet never lets his persona usurp the movie as a whole. The picture is always more important than the star.

So McGregor can function equally well as a lead, as part of an ensemble, or as a background fixture. In *Blue Juice*, *Shallow Grave* and *Velvet Goldmine* he is part of a team, and functions as such. He does not stand out from the action simply because that is not required of him. Mark Herman's *Brassed Off*, by contrast, is a more old-fashioned, less youth-targeted picture. The real drama, and the proper locus of the story, is on the father–son experiences of Pete Postlethwaite and Stephen Tompkinson. McGregor and Tara Fitzgerald are a concession to younger viewers, functioning as the youthful lovers who meet across the mining divide. The McGregor role is part of a sub-plot. It is, to date, possibly his least complex role. His French-horn playing miner is bluff, charming and likeable, but he is kept within tight narrative parameters. Again, McGregor does the job efficiently and doesn't go looking for further glory. Such an approach bespokes boundless confidence as an actor and a refreshing lack of ego.

Nor is he averse to taking risky roles. The part of Jerome, the malleable English translator in Greenaway's *The Pillow Book*, might have tripped up a lesser performer. Jerome is, in essence, a blank canvas, a man willing to forsake any personality and turn himself into the Frankenstein's experiment of a domineering Japanese calligrapher. There is no hook for the portrayal, no meat of character for an actor to get his teeth into. As a flesh-and-blood being, Jerome is only ever half there. He is a cypher, a walking art object. He serves, in the words of the film, as a 'clay model of a human being'. McGregor, nude for much of the film, was left with no disguise, no acting pyrotechnics to fall back on. In negotiating his shadowy role in *The Pillow Book*, he elected to play it as a diminished version of his true character. '*The Pillow Book* was the film where I used my voice for the first time,' he explains. 'And I found that quite exposing. It felt like

133

me. But then again it wasn't me, you know? I haven't slept with any old Japanese guys. Yet.'

Throughout *The Pillow Book*, McGregor downplays his character to an unnerving degree, until his final anguished scene. Locked out of Nagiko's room and screaming disconsolately behind the wall, he hardly seems to be emoting at all. Hair brushed back, and casual in a low-key white shirt and unbuttoned jacket, he cuts a deliberately unremarkable figure. Jerome is bemused, good-natured and content to be under the sway of others. McGregor's delivery is sometimes mumbled, sometimes self-conscious. His lines trail off faintly at the end, giving a blurred and uncertain edge to his character. In another film this might smack of weakness, of a lack of decisiveness in bringing a character to life. Here, it is just right. All vague contours and pliable flesh, Jerome proves to be beautifully in tune with the generally dislocated, elusive ambience of *The Pillow Book* as a whole.

Trainspotting posed other problems. McGregor's Renton is simultaneously the star of the film (his role beefed up from the book) and the most ordinary and everyday of its characters. Tommy is the strapping innocent who slides into addiction, Sick Boy the suave, amoral lad-about-town. Spud is a mess of amphetamine tics and twitches and Begbie is, quite simply, a monster. And all the while Renton sits in the centre, the quiet eye of the storm. Renton's only proactive gestures come towards the end of the film (his move to London, his final act of robbery). For the rest of the time he is passive, vacillating in a muted fashion to the events taking place around him. Even in his doleful pursuit of schoolgirl temptress Diane, it is she who's the one in charge. Like Martin Sheen in *Apocalypse Now*, McGregor is in place to anchor the tale. He acts as a control on the myriad indulgences going on around him.

'Looking back, I think that's probably the thing I'm most proud of,' reckons McGregor. 'There's a lot of difference between not doing anything and doing nothing,' points out Danny Boyle. 'Renton is very modern, he doesn't show much emotion, he becomes what you want him to be.' And, of course, the voice-over made it all a bit easier. Caustic, rueful and intelligent, Renton's narration both defines his character and maps out the landscape he inhabits. The voice-over almost exists as a separate character. It acts as our tour-guide. It is lively, seductive, yet never totally trustworthy.

Trainspotting stands as McGregor's most impressive achievement thus far. His performance is subtle, intense and inward-directed. Hollow-eyed and thin as a whippet, McGregor's Renton is still McGregor, but altered somehow. It's a projection of how Ewan might have turned out had he been born in Leith as opposed to Crieff; had he run with a bad crowd, had his natural charisma become cramped and misguided. Yet McGregor's native wit, charm and acting expertise mean that there is still a strange approachability to Renton. He may be a junkie. He may be weak and unreliable. He may fuck his friends over. He may be, as he describes himself, 'a bad person'. But he is also, implicitly, one of us. His take on life is our take: he makes feeble attempts to get girls into bed; he slobs about in bed leafing through a book on Montgomery Clift; he plays football – badly; he hungers for something better, but can't quite work up the energy to decide what it is, let alone go chasing it. We empathize with Renton and this empathy is crucial to *Trainspotting*. Without it the film would just be another fly-on-the-wall account of junkie low-life. With it, the viewers find themselves relating to the characters. We are bound to the drama, implicated in the story. Hodge's script and Boyle's direction lay the groundwork, but it is McGregor's performance that truly brings the tale to life.

When shooting *Trainspotting*, Boyle quickly came to see McGregor and Carlyle as the acting heavyweights in the cast:

> Ewan is very good technically. In that respect, he's like Bobby Carlyle. He's not fazed by all that technical bollocks finding your mark, finding your lights. He just absorbs it and still gives this performance that seems organic. Ewen Bremner can't do that. If he thinks about the technical side, it ruins his work.

Boyle was also impressed by McGregor's willingness to take risks with the content of his character, to be unconcerned by the prospect of looking foolish or uncool. In *A Life Less Ordinary*, McGregor switched from the lean, aloof Renton to play Robert, a banana-heeled Scottish janitor-cum-kidnapper adrift in the American Midwest. With this role, the actor brilliantly bucked audience expectations. Robert is a consciously comic character: a sweet-natured, slapstick bungler hopelessly in thrall to Cameron Diaz's spoilt little rich girl, Celine. When Robert is held at gunpoint he wails like a baby. When he and Celine first kiss, outside a convenience store, a string of saliva connects them as they break off. Movie heroes were rarely as unglamorous as this. McGregor, though, had no qualms about presenting a more dopey and inept side of his personality. 'If you were worried about looking vulnerable in a movie, it would mean you were acting about yourself,' he explains.

> To play Robert, who's very emotional and sensitive, and a little bit feminine here and there, is fine. If I were to worry about that, it would mean I was doing movies to make me look cool. And I'm really not. I'm an actor and I want to play loads of different parts, loads of different people. I don't care how they reflect on me personally, because they're not supposed to be me. So I'm not afraid to portray people who are vulnerable, because there are a lot of vulnerable people out there. I'm one myself.

Perhaps more than any other of McGregor's roles, Robert seems a contemporary overhaul of the sort of part James Stewart or Henry Fonda might have tackled fifty years earlier. It is, to date, the role that most reveals his influences.

Yet, as an actor, McGregor is as much defined by what he hates as what he likes. The current crop of Hollywood A-listers does nothing much for him, particularly such ingratiating 'youth' stars as Will Smith and Jim Carrey. Ewan notably detested *Independence Day*, the sci-fi blockbuster that made rapper-turned-TV-heart-throb Smith a star. 'Abominable,' he said. 'They should have their Equity cards taken away.'. But his real ire is reserved for Carrey, the energetic comedy mega-star whose karaoke Jerry Lewis schtick in films like *Ace Ventura: Pet Detective*, *The Mask* and *Liar, Liar* have nudged him to the top of the salary scale – charging a going rate of $20 million a film. 'I just can't watch his films,' complains McGregor. 'I just cannot fucking stomach the man. I read somewhere that Jim Carrey was saying that it's such a problem now because he is so famous he can't even leave his house without being mobbed. Well, fine. Let him stay in his house. Lock him in there!'

The $20 million mob disgusts him in general. He feels Hollywood itself is to blame. 'The industry's just gone to the extreme,' he told Kirsty Young during a Talk Radio interview in February 1998. 'Like with Demi Moore. It's ridiculous what she's up to.' Moore's perceived on-set avarice has earned her the nickname 'Gimme' Moore. On a recent shoot, there were rumours that she had demanded no less than three luxury trailers to recline in. Another wisp of gossip alleges that she once changed hotel suites because the colour scheme clashed with her outfit. Eddie Murphy, reckoned Ewan, operated in a similar fashion: 'Eddie Murphy costs film companies more than a million pounds purely for his team of people, who sit in his trailer and run around after him. It's a waste of time and money. And his films are all rubbish anyway.'

McGregor's contempt for Smith, Carrey and Murphy is significant. All three are 'personality' movie stars; famous as much for what they represent, the image they peddle, as the work that they do. All are, in a sense, the modern-day equivalent of the old Hollywood stars of the thirties and forties: reliable, easily identifiable, faintly straitjacketed by the system and forever being fitted into projects tailor-made for them. But where such actors as Grant and Stewart were graceful, canny and surprisingly versatile, actors like Carrey seem set rigid, his personality a mask which has set to his face. Smith, Carrey and Murphy appear to be products of Hollywood in its most crude, constraining form. All three are required to lean heavily on their innate charm as a substitute for rigorous acting, and all three have become multi-millionaires from following this course. For a man on the cusp of a similar level of success, it is perhaps wise that McGregor should react to such actors with distaste. Theirs is a dead-end road, which shows how end-of-the-century Hollywood can turn natural charm into a cartoonish commodity. McGregor, then, is understandably wary of Hollywood. 'The more I'm in LA the less I want to go back,' he says. 'They talk to me about a $200 million and I'm thinking, that's disgusting. I'd be lost in some big studio picture.'

Thus far those instincts have served him well. He acknowledges that he has been 'lucky' with his roles, but, inevitably, McGregor has tripped up once or twice. A few shaky jobs in a few insubstantial productions litter his CV. Early on in his career, he took a supporting slot opposite Elliott Gould (a famously wayward talent) on the BBC Screen One teleplay *Doggin' Around*.

> That was one thing I really wasn't happy with. It was a great script by Alan Plater, but it was really badly made. Just awful. But in movies I've been very fortunate. Even *Blue Juice*, which nobody really likes. I know there are problems with the film. It's split up into four stories in the middle and somehow that just doesn't

work. But I still think it's a very sweet film and I was pleased with what I did in it. I had a great time doing it and I'm pleased with what I came up with. So the film as a whole doesn't matter to me, because I still got something out of it.

Emma, however, was quite a different matter. 'Yeah, I was shit in that. But then you learn from that, too.' McGregor's role as the rakish Frank Churchill is the only movie role that has failed his 'embarrassment-factor test'. McGregor explains:

> It all depends how far down the seat you go. I was pretty far down during that. But I only saw it on tape; I didn't see it at the cinema. I was watching it with friends, going, "Oh, fuck." And I ended up behind the sofa. I just didn't believe a word I said on *Emma*. And I don't mean that as a reflection on anyone but myself. I just didn't work hard enough. I wasn't committed enough.

Admittedly, McGregor cuts an awkward figure on *Emma*, yet there are still moments when his loose, boyish charisma comes through unfettered. He is, perhaps, at his best in it when he's being most contemporary; when he breaks out of the corseted strictures of the film and becomes Ewan McGregor again. Reviewing the film in the *Sunday Telegraph*, Chris Peachment took issue with this quality, reckoning that McGregor was 'rather too modern in idiom'. The *Independent*'s Adam Mars-Jones posed a more sophisticated analysis:

> Nothing in Ewan McGregor's past life on screen [*Shallow Grave*, *Trainspotting*] would suggest his suitability for playing Frank Churchill. But the discrepancy in his acting style pays a dividend. It becomes part of the character's dangerous charm that he enters a conspiracy with the person he's talking to, as if they alone know what is real and what is not. In a genteel stratum, this raffish energy, this irony and dryness could do a lot of damage.

So, once again, McGregor wriggles free from the critics' condemnation, if not his own. As an actor, he seems possessed of the Midas touch. Put him in a good film and he leaps further up the movie-star ladder. Put him in a poor one and he is somehow seen to subvert it, to grace it with some of his reflected glory, to include his audience by making them co-conspirators in his own discomfort. Nudging into his late twenties, McGregor, has hit that rare and enviable stage when success breeds further success, when he can literally do no wrong. Such remorseless momentum might intimidate most professional players, but McGregor appears to take it all deliciously in his stride. If anything, success has loosened him up and liberated his confidence in his innate talents.

Despite his insistence that he remains a 'vulnerable person', Ewan McGregor gives the impression of being extremely comfortable with being a celebrity. While other actors use their roles as a screen, he employs them as a showcase – a spotlight on the various aspects of his character. Whether he be caustic, cynical, genial, bumbling, witty, sexy, sussed, bewildered, cocky, coarse or sophisticated, each trait comes across as authentic and organic. There is no Method rage in his mode of working, and, considering his reputation as Britain's hippest star, he is an actor almost entirely free from angst. His perfor- mances are driven by an easy grace. His charisma is of the crumpled, unself-conscious variety, worlds away from the jut-jawed narcissism that typifies so many movie stars. If McGregor is vulnerable, he seems remarkably at ease with that vulnerability:

> The Scots are an emotional race. My mother will cry at the drop of a hat, usually with joy, though. I cry easily, too, and so does my dad. But in America men appear to feel they need to be macho. That's partly why British actors seem more interesting to them.

Danny Boyle elaborates:

I think Ewan's got this thing that Michael Caine has. It's that next-door quality. If you break it down, neither of them is Brad Pitt good-looking, but they are both very sexy. Like Caine in the early days, Ewan can hold a movie without a blazing, blazing performance; all that acting madness. They trust the movie to follow them. They don't go chasing it.

● ● ● ● ●

As an actor, Ewan McGregor proves a pretty polymorphic customer. He slides casually out of easy-fit pigeonholes and never stays still long enough to have a label slapped on him. Junkie icon, *objet d'art*, period rake, bungling kidnapper – the man's roles already run a terrific gamut. They are all him and yet not him, and he is defined by none of them. His influences are old-school, resolutely unfashionable; his bearing is as current as the day. He is that rare creature, a bona fide British movie star who remains an actor first and foremost; a headline star content to play second fiddle when the need demands. He takes his work seriously, yet a lively wit seems to be forever dancing in the wings. His core motivation for acting, he told one interviewer, is 'fear of being crap'. But there is no evidence of fear, no perceivable inhibition in the films of Ewan McGregor. He takes ceaseless risks and gets away with them, adapts himself smoothly to each new challenge. In a world of artifice and hypocrisy, he steers his own course and remains his own man. And what could be more powerful than that?

McGREGOR THE STYLE OBJECT

8. McGREGOR THE STYLE OBJECT

'Britain is kicking off again,' Ewan McGregor told *Empire* magazine at the end of 1997. 'And I am very happy to be a part of it.'

Track back from the close-up and it becomes immediately clear that Ewan McGregor is a part of something much bigger than the mechanics of each individual performance. He has become hooked into some wider trend, some grass-roots swell. Talent takes the lion's share of the credit, but his pole position in British culture has a lot to do with fate too. Put it down to the accident of birth. Had he been born a year or two earlier, or a year or two later, he might not be in the place he is today. As it is, he is young enough, gifted enough and untainted enough by past history to be regarded as a child of the turning millennium. Ewan McGregor's biological birthdate was the spring of 1971. In cultural terms he was born on 23 February 1996, the day that saw the domestic release of Danny Boyle's *Trainspotting*. At that time, Oasis were topping the charts with 'Don't Look Back in Anger'; the Tory government was slouching towards the last twelve months of a spent and discredited term in office. It was to be an era of change; the dawn of a bright new tomorrow looming large.

That same year, America's *Newsweek* ran its now-famous catch-all overview of the British arts scene, claiming its upswing as a signifier of a resurgent society. The phrase they coined – now stale from over-use – was Cool Britannia (formerly a line in a song by the Bonzo Dog Doodah Band, latterly a brand of Ben and Jerry's ice-cream). At the hub of this upswing was London – swinging in the sixties, floundering in the seventies, split between the haves and have-nots in the eighties but now, so *Newsweek* reckoned, hip and happening once more. All areas of popular culture showed the signs of this new vitality. Art had been invigorated by the arrival of maverick players like Damien Hirst, Tracey Emin and Sarah Lucas; literature by writers like Irvine Welsh, Alex Garland and Alan Warner. But it was in music, always the most inclusive and youth-orientated of all the arts, that the renaissance was most felt. As it did in the sixties, pop music serves as our culture's most immediate form of expression, the most accurate barometer of collective cultural health. In the eighties, pop music was either marginalized or marketed to death. The era was characterized by a seemingly irrevocable split. The charts were monopolized by chill, manufactured produce (as typified by the Stock, Aitken and Waterman stable). The more challenging alternative sounds were slotted away in the indie ghetto, unwilling or unable to connect with a wider audience.

A thaw set in during the late eighties with the commercial success of Manchester bands like the Stone Roses and the Happy Mondays. The music of both bands – a heady hybrid sixties pop and seventies funk – was sufficiently approachable to dent the charts, but edgy and attitudinal enough to stick close to its working-class youth roots. Paralleling this rise came the developments in dance music: a trend similarly rooted in Manchester's inner-city club and warehouse environment. This, in turn, spawned Ecstasy culture and the rave scene which brought together a disparate cross-section of home-grown youth – from indie kids to ex-hippies, disco throwbacks to pop tarts – under one unifying banner. Not since the days of punk had such an organic and grass-roots phenomenon swept through the cities of Britain.

The nineties have seen these new forms of music grow steadily more legitimate and become more a part of society's mainstream. But they still have the snap of something fresh and volatile about them. After their breakthrough debut album in 1989, the Stone Roses virtually dropped out of sight for five years, ostensibly to record their follow-up ('one year to record the album, four years in bed,' admitted Mani the bass-player). But on their return (with *The Second Coming* in 1994) the landscape had changed, and they were no longer leading the pack. The intervening years had seen the Roses' and Mondays' influence filter through to a whole host of other bands. Brit-pop looked both to these immediate ancestors and further back, to the classic pop songs of sixties artists like the Rolling Stones, the Kinks and, particularly, the Beatles. Blur had first grazed the charts in 1991 with their wannabe 'Madchester' riff 'There's No Other Way'. By 1994 they were arguably England's most important band. Their *Park Life* album proved a bracing update on the Kinks' London-life portraiture, complete with a canny 'New Lad' swagger.

Pulp had been going even longer. Initially formed in the New Romantic days of 1980, they belatedly rose to the fore during the mid-nineties. By this time frontman Jarvis Cocker was pushing thirty-three, but his spry, post-adolescent vignettes ('Disco 2000', 'Common People') struck a rousing chord with the teen set. Completing the trio was Oasis: straight out of Manchester and the most influenced by that city's cultural spell in the sun (the young Liam Gallagher had idolized the Stone Roses' frontman Ian Brown; brother Noel had roadied for

Madchester nearly-weres the Inspiral Carpets). Blending nineties abrasiveness with wholesale lifts from late sixties-era Beatles, Oasis quickly established themselves as the lords of the Brit-pack scene, seeing off arch-rivals Blur in the album wars of late 1995.

Fortunately, the British music scene runs deeper and wider than three leading bands. Away from the Pulp–Oasis–Blur trio, the list runs on and on. The Brit-pop canopy includes Elastica, Suede, Sleeper, Echobelly, Menswear, Cornershop, the Charlatans and the Verve (whose *Urban Hymns* was generally held to be the finest album of 1997). In the meantime, the late eighties dance scene has similarly spread and diversified, embracing such acts as Leftfield, Massive Attack, Tricky, Portishead, and the Chemical Brothers. America, struggling in a post-grunge desert, has nothing on British music in the 1990s.

The sounds of modern-day Britain ring loud in the trio of films which Ewan McGregor has made with Danny Boyle, John Hodge and Andrew Macdonald. Both *Shallow Grave* and *Trainspotting* lean heavily on home-grown music, using its sound as a touchstone for their own style and intentions. It acts as a point of reference, plus a means of mainlining the young cinema-going public. The first thing we hear in *Shallow Grave* is a Leftfield track thrumming deep behind the action, muscling the camera forward. One year later the *Trainspotting* soundtrack album proved a best-seller by interspersing a few old favourites (Lou Reed, Iggy Pop) with the best of current British talent (Primal Scream, Pulp, Elastica, Blur's Damon Albarn). And playing out *A Life Less Ordinary* we have Oasis's knees-up anthem 'Round Are Way', the B-side of their 'Wonderwall' single.

Fittingly, Cool Britannia's hottest movie star is most fond of Cool Britannia's most successful pop band. Ewan McGregor has been partial to Oasis ever since he caught 'Cigarettes and Alcohol' on the radio back in 1994. In his teenage years, he would sing Billy Idol songs before setting off for school in the mornings. These days he'll stick Oasis on the headphones. 'I never had a band I was fanatical about when I was a kid and, rather embarrassingly, it happened when I was twenty-four, twenty-five, with Oasis.'

He is on decent, semi-friendship terms with the band, hanging out with them after an appearance on American TVs *Saturday Night Live*. 'Champagne Supernova' is one particular favourite; their number-one single 'Some Might Say' another. But Ewan is not averse to other bands of the current scene. During John Hodge's wedding reception in 1997, he took to the mike for a live rendition of Pulp's 'Common People', a doubly ironic anthem when one considers the singer and the company he keeps.

Although McGregor was always geared towards acting, he still carries a torch for his sideline musical ambitions; those heady days drumming for Scarlet Pride or busking in the tube during his time at Guildhall. 'I always wanted to be a rock star. I don't think anything can compare to the buzz you get playing in front of a live audience. Not theatre, certainly. It's a fucking primal thing, I guess.'

He inadvertently realized this desire when his introductory *Trainspotting* monologue was sampled by London-based musical collective, the PF Project, who choreographed his words to an urgent, trancey beat. Approached by the outfit, McGregor listened to the backing track and gave his permission to lift his speech wholesale. 'Choose Life', by the PF Project and Ewan McGregor, reached number six in the UK charts towards the end of 1997. But, if he can't be a legitimate rock star, Ewan's day job affords him the next best thing. In 1998 he cropped up as an Iggy Pop-style performer in Todd Haynes's glam-rock saga *Velvet Goldmine*.

Herein lies the key allure of acting: providing Ewan with the opportunity to sample the lives and careers that might have been.

If pop music traditionally serves as the pioneer of cultural rebirth, cinema can't help but lag a little way behind. Where music can be birthed by a few super-keen boys with electronic toys or a second-hand set of decks, shooting film tends to be a more complex, collaborative and big-business enterprise. A script is written, gets passed around the money men and – if deemed suitable – is then put into 'development' where it can languish unused for years. The nature of the beast works against spontaneity, against risk, against experimentation. Film, for better or worse, is a collaborative medium. Or, as American writer and sometime director David Mamet puts it: 'Film is a collaborative medium – bend over.'

In terms of cultural impact, film is always chasing the front-runners. Pop music points the way, articulates the culture, frames the lifestyle and exports a sense of grass-roots Britishness around the globe. 'Our films are beginning to do that,' argues Danny Boyle, 'though pop music's hold on the culture is still stronger.'

But if there is one film that has come close to catching the latent energy and immediacy of modern British culture it is *Trainspotting*. In its rapacious portrait of Leith's junkie sub-strata, it seemed to burst forth to frame a 'spot in time'. There was no tell-tale sense of time-lag to the film. Like the perfect pop song, it gave the impression of creating itself as it played, of defining itself and its milieu as the celluloid unrolled in front of the viewer. This is a tribute to Welsh's source novel, to Hodge's devastating adaptation, to Boyle's direction and, indeed, to the performances of all concerned. But it is also something of an illusion. For *Trainspotting* is a tightly packaged, highly marketed product. It is simply that the packaging was so deftly done, and so snugly in tune with the nihilistic aspirations of its target audience, that we find ourselves scarcely aware of the in-your-face hard sell that underlies the film.

The marketing of *Trainspotting* amounts to a kind of advertising genius. The ground was mapped out from the start. The heroin-themed story was controversial and contentious. But, if handled intelligently, its taboo topic needn't be offputting to a general audience. Drugs had become a way of life among vast sections of British youth. The drug-taking experience was being articulated in music and, increasingly, in literature, and yet film still had to tap into the trend. In this light, Macdonald's project seemed to be presented with something of an open goal. Whether the execution was good or ill, a certain level of press attention was guaranteed. *Trainspotting* would, at the very least, merit a footnote in the annals of British cinema history.

In the weeks leading up to release, the advertising campaign trod a brilliantly sure-footed course. First, there was that eye-catching cinema trailer, which abandoned the usual means of splicing together various taster segments from the feature in favour of a specially made 'short': the *Trainspotting* gang astride a railway track. Running parallel came the poster campaign of jaw-dropping inspiration. By placing the key cast members side by side in aggressive glamour poses, the posters pulled off an audacious balancing act. On the one hand, they posited *Trainspotting*'s dead-beat squadron as cool lifestyle accessories, to be snapped up by savvy consumers the nation over. On the other, they gave a sly nod to the inherent crassness of such a technique by exaggerating it to the point of parody. The five principals (Begbie, Diane, Sick Boy, Spud and Renton) were even numbered, as though each served as designs on a trump card – components of a kit to be collected and fitted lovingly together.

Meanwhile the oft-quoted monologue which kicks off the narrative

('Choose life, choose a job, choose a career . . .' etc.) seems consciously set up as a kind of pastiche of traditional ad-speak. This kind of sloganeering blather is the life-blood of insurance commercials on TV, or the back-to-work pamphlets you might flick through in the DSS queue. Again, the mantra serves a dual purpose: simultaneously debunking the dictates of the hard sell and subtly honouring it. Because, at the bottom line, the *Trainspotting* campaign is peddling something. First and foremost it promotes the film itself. The film, in turn, is pushing a certain lifestyle. All movies sell a certain lifestyle, a certain aesthetic. What *Trainspotting* sells is youth, insouciance, distrust of the system, a cool-chip strain of nihilism.

All of which gives rise to a classic paradox: the selling of rebellion and non-conformity to the widest possible audience. *Trainspotting* gets around it brilliantly. Realizing that its target audience is sussed enough to know that ad-speak lies – and is in many ways the dead language of a discredited system – *Trainspotting* proceeds to frame itself with a kind of anti-ad ad-campaign, one that is louchely knowing, shrewdly self-referential. As an example of youth-targeting this is sophisticated in the extreme. Yet it is still, at the bottom line, advertising at work. The trappings may change, the core intention remains the same.

The poster campaign was also aided by its featured models: hard-nut Begbie, funny-bloke Spud, and the pointed, perfect prettiness of Diane, Sick Boy and Renton. In the early posters, the figure of Renton was merely one of the team, reflecting the more ensemble sweep of Welsh's novel. In later prints he came to dominate. Today the poster image of *Trainspotting*'s 'junkie sex god' (in the words of *Time Out*) has become a *de rigueur* decoration for student dorm rooms and twentysomething bedsits the land over. It is an iconic image. McGregor stands in hugging T-shirt, arms folded, a flash of bare belly exposed.

He's guarded, vulnerable, but still sexy. He is dripping wet – from his dive into the bookie's toilet as it turns out – but it could just as well be sweat. He looks like he's just wandered out of a fantastic club night, hugging himself as he stands in a chill grey dawn.

The look McGregor sports in *Trainspotting* inevitably taps into concerns about heroin chic. This style was pioneered by fashion photographer David Sorrenti (who later died of an overdose) and presented by models like Kate Moss, Jodie Kidd and, surely most notoriously, Versace clotheshorse Amy Wesson, who was sued by her fashion agency after an alleged heroin addiction began to impact on her work. The smack-chic look is pale, gaunt, soulful and haunted; robust, rosy youth left to wither on the vine. What the image communicates is the nearness of death in the prime of life, and this is nothing new. Heroin chic is just the latest manifestation of the studied fatalism previously showcased by seventies punk (with its no-future mantra) and eighties Goth (vampire costumes; powder-cake make-up). On this occasion, the direct connection with class-A drugs made it all a shade more volatile. In May 1997 President Clinton lashed out at the heroin-chic image which he saw as pioneered and propagated by fashion magazines, damning it for making drug use seem 'glamorous, sexy and cool. The glorification of heroin is not creative, it's destructive,' Clinton continued. 'It's not beauty, it's ugly. This is not about art, it's about life and death. And glorifying death is not good for society.'

McGregor, though, has no qualms about how *Trainspotting* makes him appear. He told *Neon* magazine:

> It was a good look. It's a cracking look. And they're good pictures. So I don't care at all . . . It is sexy because it represents danger, and a life that most of us wouldn't lead. People either decided to be frightened of things we don't know

about, or excited by them. So on that level it makes sense that it's an attracting look. And I'm wet. It's a wet T-shirt! So that's good. We all like a wet T-shirt, don't we?

The *Trainspotting* role marked Ewan McGregor in the public imagination. He became iconic, the symbol for a generation in much the way Brando was in *The Wild One*, or Malcolm McDowell in Lindsay Anderson's *If*. He embodied drugged, disaffected, self-interested, intelligent Britain and gave a fledgling cultural trend the flesh-and-blood heft of life. No matter what else he does in his career, it will probably be *Trainspotting* that trails him to his grave.

● ● ● ● ●

Happily, though, McGregor has been able to move on. The three films that he made surrounding *Trainspotting* (*The Pillow Book*, *Emma*, *Brassed Off*) effectively distanced the actor from his most abiding role. As a young performer thrust abruptly into the limelight, he responded with a swift display of versatility that singled him out as a great actor as opposed to merely a blinding one-off. In particular, *The Pillow Book* deftly muddied the water. Greenaway's film transformed McGregor into an elusive and unreadable enigma. It turned the deadbeat junkie into an art-house muse. His sexuality became ambiguous, leading the *Gay Times* to comment that 'Ewan McGregor has all it takes to be the gay pin-up of the year'. *The Pillow Book* blurred Ewan McGregor. As a fluid, functioning actor, it was probably the best thing he could have done.

Even so, McGregor, with his informal grace and approachable good looks, still represents something that our culture covets. It would be all too easy for him to take the corporate quid and make a bundle on commercials or lucrative formula movies tailor-made to showcase his appeal. As it is, his commercial forays have been few and far between. Fresh out of Guildhall, he employed his clear-water Perthshire tones to the voice-over on a St Ivel Gold advert. More recently he has cropped up on Japanese TV, plugging Bobson jeans and a fizzy drink. 'It's called Beatnik. It's pronounced "beat-a-nik-a". It's a brown, seriously carbonated sparkling guarana drink.' The yen, he reckons, is a powerful temptation:

> It's about large amounts of money. That's the beauty of Japanese commercials; they're only shown in Japan. I would never do a commercial here. I've been offered Calvin Klein ads and shit like that. But when I see an actor do a fashion ad in a magazine I'm always just a wee bit disappointed.

He can, however, be heard as the voice of the suave (and a just a shade camp) cabin-class host (opposite Leslie Phillips's twirly-moustached pilot) on Virgin Atlantic's in-flight instruction movie. 'My voice-over agents are from ages ago,' he confessed to the *Face*. 'I love them to death. So I do stuff for them. Perhaps it's because I'm stupid.' As with the *Trainspotting* campaign, McGregor attempts to give the impression that such ventures have a tongue-in-cheek quality to them, a sly take on consumerism in general.

Otherwise, Ewan McGregor has more serious matters on his mind. Following *Trainspotting*, he found himself at the vanguard of a new generation of British talent. 'Ewan is in the position now that his name can open a movie,' points out Danny Boyle. 'That's rare for a British actor; you can probably count the others on the finger of one hand. Maybe Robert Carlyle is another one.'

Carlyle, of course, used his *Trainspotting* stint as a springboard to the major league. On-set the two men anchored one another; the match-up of laid-back Renton and bristling Begbie was one of the film's key dynamics – one which subtly paralleled Renton's equally uneasy friendship with heroin. But off-camera the two men are not particularly close. Ten years older, Carlyle apparently sometimes found himself at a distance from the crew camaraderie on the film's set. McGregor, for his part, found he got on best with Jonny Lee Miller who is more similar in age, outlook and background.

Since shooting wrapped the two men have become fast friends whose circle in London includes Jude Law, Sadie Frost and Sean Pertwee (who all worked together in *Shopping*). For a time the crowd all lived within a mile radius of each other in Primrose Hill. When their respective schedules coincided they would throw epic parties at one or other of their flats. These days the emphasis has shifted and matters have grown more businesslike. In 1997 the five young guns, with producers Damon Bryant and Brad Adams in tow, announced the launch of Natural Nylon, an independent production company dedicated to developing the best of young British scripts. Based in a small suite of offices in Soho, Natural Nylon takes its lead from the guiding principles of United Artists, the breakaway of film production company formed in 1919 by DW Griffith, Mary Pickford, Douglas Fairbanks and Charlie Chaplin. It is a means of letting the performers take charge of their own destiny, of wresting control from the money men. With Natural Nylon, Ewan McGregor effectively joins their ranks. He becomes a film producer and prospective director. Mogul status beckons.

● ● ● ● ●

McGregor's mates may have a southern bias, but the man himself suggests evidence of an increasing northern takeover in British culture. He heads a Scottish phalanx of actors that includes Carlyle, *Four Weddings* and *Sliding Doors* star John Hannah and Joe McFadden, the star of Gillies MacKinnon's *Small Faces* and the BBC adaptation of Iain Banks's *The Crow Road*.

That Scotland is in vogue is hard to dispute. In many ways the country has now usurped Ireland, traditionally viewed in the public imagination as the stronghold of the Celtic soul. Perhaps it has something to do with a reaction against the traditional RSC pedigree of English acting, the tell-tale class in the accent, or in the bearing, that works against the more gritty aspects of modern British storytelling. One theory of why Scottish performers are so popular at present, and export so well, is that very few people in the average audience can distinguish the class permutations in the Scots accent. Scotland has become a cultural shorthand for authenticity, for classlessness. Inevitably this is a huge misconception. Ewan McGregor, for one, is as middle class as they come. As it is, he has become arguably Scotland's most successful acting export since Sean Connery, the tax-exile Bond icon whom Sick Boy so obsessed over throughout *Trainspotting*. 'I would say in those days that he was a muscular actor,' muses Sick Boy on Connery's Bond heyday, 'with all the presence of someone like Cooper or Lancaster, but combined with a sly wit to make him a formidable romantic lead. Closer in that respect to Cary Grant.' Such sentiments can now be applied to McGregor.

Nestled at the heart of *Trainspotting* is a classic piece of anti-Scots invective. 'I hate Scotland,' quips Renton, hunched cold and weary on the edge of the Pentlands. 'We're the lowest of the fucking low, the scum of the earth. The most wretched, servile, miserable, pathetic trash that was ever shat into civilization. Some people hate the English. I don't. They're just wankers. We, on the other hand, are colonized by wankers. We can't even pick a decent culture to be colonized by.'

McGregor looks back on Renton's speech with amusement:

His anger against the English, but more than that, his anger against the Scots for putting up with it in the first place, is something I can really relate to. The Tories introduced the Poll Tax in Scotland before they did anywhere else. And what did we do? We marched and we moaned about it. But when they introduced it in England there were riots on the streets and they had to repeal it. Scottish people are good at complaining.

Nowadays, of course, the situation is changing. Scotland is empowering itself, pushing for self rule as part of a gradual decentralization of power away from Westminster. In the meantime, the current Labour administration bears a heavily Scottish representation, with Robin Cook (Foreign Secretary) and Gordon Brown (Chancellor of the Exchequer) occupying the second two most powerful posts in the British government. In terms of cultural impact, Scotland's time has arrived.

Conversely, McGregor himself inhabits a jumbled and cosmopolitan landscape. While fiercely, colourfully Scottish, he has slotted himself seamlessly into the scene in London (which he salutes 'the best fucking city in the world'). He is also married to a Frenchwoman and feels most akin to the culture in rural France. 'I know France has got problems, too,' he admits. 'Fucking Chirac, for instance. But I really get off on that lifestyle. Drinking Pastis in a little village bar. Playing a game of boules with the old chaps. It just seems a very civilized way to live.' An eventual move to France is one that he's been considering for years. 'I might buy a house out there at some point,' he says wryly. 'If I make any money from acting in movies.'

As a rising young actor, and the star of the era's most zeitgeist-defining British film, Ewan McGregor inevitably finds himself at the hub of whatever cultural resurgence is presently occurring in the country. It is a time that bears inevitable parallels with 'swinging sixties' London. The current London arts scene is young, vital and oddly interconnected, predominantly strung out around a few drinking haunts in Soho. As with the sixties, there is an intimate, village feel to this scene, at least in the popular imagination and in the depiction of a London-centric media: the sense that everybody knows each other.

At the tail end of 1997, the *Independent on Sunday* ran a lifestyle piece comparing modern London with the city of thirty years earlier. Each aspect had its mirror image, its cultural ancestor. Ewan McGregor, reckoned the paper, was most akin to sixties icon David Hemmings, the star of Michelangelo Antonioni's voguish London thriller *Blow Up*. But this seems a backhanded compliment and one which implicitly hints at future dangers for McGregor. For Hemmings was an actor of a specific moment in time, inextricably bound to one era. After *Blow Up*, he faded from the scene.

This is the downside of McGregor's particular brand of success, of becoming the conduit for an entire arts scene. Fashionability can become a prison. This year's model can become next year's antique. It remains to be seen whether McGregor can escape his time before it turns sour, and whether his persona and acting abilities are evergreen and adaptable enough to address the lifestyle and issues of subsequent eras and new audiences. For chameleon players like De Niro, Day-Lewis, and even Robert Carlyle, this is never such a concern. But McGregor is the closest that a jobbing actor can get to being a rock star or a catwalk model. Moving with the times will be his next big challenge.

The chances are that McGregor will be OK. Even this early on in his career, he has proved himself bigger than any individual role, able to vary the tempo and change the tone of his playing. He has remained discriminating, mobile and alert. And yet at the same time he has turned iconic – a symbol of the age. For better or worse, Ewan McGregor has become stitched into the fabric of our culture.

A LIFE LESS ORDINARY

9. A LIFE LESS ORDINARY

A backlash, of course, was inevitable. 'It's the British way, isn't it?' reflected McGregor ruefully. 'Build 'em up and knock 'em down. It was just our turn to catch the flak, that's all.'

What, exactly, went wrong with *A Life Less Ordinary*? Was it simply a case, as McGregor contends, of mean British ethics; unrealistic expectations; the hype bubble bursting? Or was the film itself fatally flawed and misguided, a worrying creative fumble after the casual triumphs of *Shallow Grave* and *Trainspotting*?

The third film from the Boyle–Hodge–Macdonald stable emerged after a lengthy gestation period. Hodge had an embryonic draft of the script on his word processor back in 1993. He wrote it at a sprint, soon after putting the finishing touches to *Shallow Grave* and eager to turn his hand to something different. The two screenplays were like chalk and cheese. Where *Shallow Grave* was dark and claustrophobic, this tale of a kidnapper and his captive was sunny and spacious. Where the first was pinned down by a strict, straightforward plot-line, the second ran a broad gamut of themes and styles, its tone as changeable as summer weather in the Highlands.

A Life Less Ordinary stands as Hodge's most ambitious and personal screenwriting exercise. From the outset, it lacked the straight genre co-ordinates that helped sustain *Shallow Grave*, or the source novel that served as a reference point for *Trainspotting*. This flighty, mercurial tale cast him adrift as a writer.

As such, the script-to-screen process was slow and arduous: 'One step forward, two steps back,' as Hodge put it. The writer reckons that his callow initial manuscript went through no fewer than eighteen overhauls, each one closely scrutinized by Andrew Macdonald. *Shallow Grave* got in the way fleetingly, and then the whole *Trainspotting* madness sidelined the project for a time. But, all the while, *A Life Less Ordinary* was evolving and reinventing itself. Initially the film was to open in Scotland, then proceed into rural France for the bulk of the action. It was to be a Euro-centric project: *A Year in Provence* played as an abduction thriller.

Midway through the rewrite stage, Macdonald surmised that the setting wasn't quite right. The film's abiding impression, it seemed, more called to mind the screwball escapades of forties Hollywood, and would subsequently sit awkwardly in the heart of France. Moreover, Hodge's narrative bristled with guns, gangster-style behaviour and the overt split between the haves (the captive and her family) and the have-nots (the kidnapper). The more Macdonald thought about it, the more unavoidable it became. *A Life Less Ordinary* needed open highways, blue skies, epic scenery and a certain youthful, pioneering spirit. America was the film's obvious host nation.

And so the script snapped neatly into place. The movie's hero would be Robert, a slack American janitor who inadvertently abducts Celine, the rich-bitch daughter of a Lionel Barrymore-esque tycoon. The pair set off across the Midwest together, Celine calling the shots, Robert stumbling bewilderedly behind. Meanwhile, watching over our two principals, are a pair of hustling, pro-active angels charged with triggering a romance between this most unlikely of couples. Rural France and Scotland looked out of the equation for good. Or so the team assumed at the time.

Later, there was one testy moment when it looked as if *A Life Less Ordinary* was destined to go down as one of the great unfilmed spectaculars. Although the project was scheduled in as the trio's third film from as early as the summer of 1994, the turbulent success of *Trainspotting* threatened to blow such carefully laid plans clean out of the water. All of a sudden the team was deluged with offers. Hodge, flush from his Oscar-nomination, received a bundle of lucra-tive offers to move from regular medicine to become a Hollywood script doctor. He was offered stints rewriting the screenplay for a proposed *Superman* movie, as well as an opportunity to pen the script for an overhaul of the seventies blax-ploitation classic, *Shaft*. Ewan McGregor was fielding offers from both sides of the Atlantic, and Boyle and Macdonald were called into meetings with Twentieth Century-Fox. The upshot of these encounters was that Boyle was offered a fee – apparently just shy of $1 million – to helm *Alien Resurrection*, the fourth instalment in the Sigourney Weaver sci-fi horror series, budgeted at a whopping $70 million. For a man used to working on limited finances, in theatre, on TV or in the strictured world of British cinema, this must have been a powerful bait.

For a few tense moments *Alien Resurrection* looked set to spell the end of the Boyle–Hodge–Macdonald troika. These days Boyle insists that this was never the case:

> When I weighed it up it just didn't grab me. It would have been a challenge, sure, but I'm not sure I really believed in the film, and it's fatal going into a big

project with that suspicion lurking in your mind. Basically I don't think I would have made it very well.

In the event, the job would fall to another rising European. Frenchman Jean-Pierre Jeunet had co-directed the giddyingly inventive art-house capers *Delicatessen* and *The City of Lost Children*, both much-praised crossover hits in Britain and America. He seemed a good enough choice, yet ultimately *Alien Resurrection* fell rather flat: it was a dour, claustrophobic and po-faced affair. In retrospect, Danny Boyle did well to steer clear of the project.

While not on the level of *Alien Resurrection*, the team's third foray nonetheless marked a big jump up the money ladder. *Shallow Grave* was budgeted at a shade over a million; *Trainspotting* at £1.7 million. *A Life Less Ordinary*, though, came in at a hefty $12 million (around £7.5 million) – small in Hollywood terms, but a whopping sum by the subsistence standards of British cinema. All of which necessitated some slick financial dealings on the part of Macdonald, who explained at the time:

> We knew Channel 4 couldn't finance the entire $12 million budget that we needed. But we wanted them to be involved because they had been so support-ive in the past. We sold them a licence for the UK television rights which gave us enough of a cash advance to go to America for location scouting and to find other backers. Our aim was to retain complete creative control over the film by retaining ownership of the negative ourselves and only offering fixed-term licences to financiers. The companies we eventually struck a deal with were PolyGram, who will distribute the film in the UK, France, Germany, Benelux, Spain, Australia and New Zealand, and Twentieth Century-Fox, who will take the US and the remainder of the world.

By all accounts Macdonald's cocksure attitude and hard-ball approach ruffled a few feathers in Hollywood. Trade Bible *Variety* marvelled at the young Brits' audacious demands and disregard of the traditional film-biz etiquette, particularly bearing in mind their relatively scant track record. Honed by years in the scramble-for-funds pool of home-grown film-making, the Brit-brat approach was now making ripples across the water.

Having bashed out a satisfactory deal, the team turned to the casting. Hodge claims that he had always written the lead character of Robert with Ewan McGregor specifically in mind. Swirling rumours that at one stage Brad Pitt was in line for the part are strenuously denied. Of their three collaborations, Hodge reckons that Robert is the role most similar to McGregor's off-screen persona: genial, scatterbrained and effortlessly charming. But after *Trainspotting*, McGregor's stock had shot through the roof. He had made *Emma* and *Brassed Off*. He had travelled to Ireland to star as a landscape gardener opposite Greta Scacchi's aristo in Philippe Rouselot's seventeenth-century mystery play *The Serpent's Kiss*. By the time *A Life Less Ordinary* went into pre-production he was in Los Angeles on the set of his first American picture. *Nightwatch* proved a bungled remake of a 1995 Danish thriller and cast McGregor as a morgue night-watchman suspected of being a serial killer. Nick Nolte and Patricia Arquette were also on the cast list, and McGregor got a chance to try out his American accent.

In the midst of filming, Boyle and Macdonald paid him a visit. They showed him Hodge's script and talked over the possibility of him playing Robert, having checked out how he was fixed over the next few months. Before they left, McGregor played them some of the rushes from *Nightwatch* to show them just how good his US accent had become. Then producer and director hopped on a plane back to England. 'They left it a couple of days and didn't phone me,' McGregor remembers. 'I thought: "Fucking hell, what's going on here?" Then they called me and said they would like me to do it.' In the meantime, the script had changed again. Following their meeting with the actor, Macdonald and Boyle consulted Hodge and the three had a rapid rethink. If McGregor was to take the lead, then that character had to be altered. Robert, in other words, had to become Scottish again. 'The American accent didn't wash with them,' shrugged Ewan. 'And I was really hurt because I thought I was doing it OK.'

With this final decision, Hodge's script for *A Life Less Ordinary* became fixed in place: if fixed is the right term for so skittish, lively and unclassifiable a picture. From the outset, *A Life Less Ordinary* broke from the inner-city blues of *Shallow Grave* and *Trainspotting* and steered its own madcap course. In most respects it is a hugely different style of picture, though Boyle, Hodge and Macdonald are quick to point out one crucial parallel. For them, this film marks the final instalment in what the team refers to as its 'bag of money trilogy'. As with the two previous pictures, a sack of loot plays a pivotal role within the narrative. It is how each film moves out from this anchor, though, that defines its eventual tone. In *A Life Less Ordinary*, the crucial kidnapping becomes the premise for something rather more sunny. Hodge explains:

> Although the reality of kidnap is pretty brutal and murderous, what I wanted to do was use it as a device, a conceit, within which to explore a romantic relationship. The rest of the story grew incrementally out of that.

What a strange breed of story this turned out to be. If *Shallow Grave* and *Trainspotting* are the equivalent of the perfect three-minute pop song – lean, hard and fast – *A Life Less Ordinary* comes on as a kind of cinematic prog-rock album: full of extravagant solos and wacky conceptual riffs. Aside from the tale's on-the-run twosome, Hodge stirs in an audacious divine-intervention sub-plot in which the Archangel Gabriel dispatches two lackies to Earth to act as strong-arm cupids. The makers even planned to include a cameo from God in the film; a decision that would probably have landed the film in as much hot water as *Trainspotting*. The trouble came in finding an actor of the required weight and stature. Marlon Brando was one suggestion; Charlton Heston another. Sean Connery was offered the part but declined (even though, he insisted, he remained a big fan of *Trainspotting*). Another name bandied about was Martin Scorsese. Danny Boyle moved quickly to crush this suggestion. 'Directors all think they're God anyway,' he quipped. The casting of the Almighty became something of a parlour game for the film-makers, then a source of irritation, and finally a distraction. In the end, the film's finale was rewritten. God was given the boot.

Other slots proved easier to fill. Boyle and Macdonald had little connection with the American industry, but an encounter with top Stateside casting agent Donna Issacson proved a major boon. With her help, they were able to cast grim-faced character actor Dan Hedaya as a five-o'clock-shadowed Angel Gabriel, *Big Night* creator Stanley Tucci as Celine's crazed dentist lover and stage and screen actor Tony Shalhoub in a pivotal role as a bartender. British veteran Ian McNeice came on board as the butler, and Ian Holm, fresh from starring in Atom Egoyan's marvellous *The Sweet Hereafter,* was roped in as Mr Neville, the rapacious capitalist who is Celine's father and Robert's boss. In terms of screen time, these was not major roles. But after *Trainspotting*, the team was in demand. Actors were clamouring to find a prestigious niche in the follow-up project.

For the roles of Jackson and O'Reilly, the tale's two hard-arse angels, Boyle went with chrome-domed Delroy Lindo, whose work he had admired in Spike Lee's *Crooklyn* and *Clockers,* and Holly Hunter, whom he had met at that year's Cannes Film Festival (he was there with *Trainspotting,* she with David

Cronenberg's controversial *Crash*). 'Very often I choose projects based on my impressions of the director,' Hunter explains, 'and Danny was no exception to that rule. I looked at *A Life Less Ordinary* solely because of his involvement.'

The co-starring part of Celine posed more of a problem. Various actresses were screen-tested; all were found wanting. The role was tricky to master. Celine must be spiky, spoilt, frequently callous and yet still loveable. In many respects she comes across as a figure from an earlier age, a throwback to the take-charge heroines epitomized by stars like Katharine Hepburn, Irene Dunne and Barbara Stanwyck. Her infuriating, contradictory nature appeared beyond the talents of the current generation of women stars. Eventually Boyle hit on Cameron Diaz, the twenty-two-year-old rising star of *The Mask* (opposite McGregor's much-detested Jim Carrey) and the duff Keanu Reeves drama, *Feeling Minnesota*. 'It sounds cheesy,' says Boyle, 'but as soon as she walked in the room I knew she was right.' Most importantly, Boyle reckoned the actress would get on well with McGregor. *A Life Less Ordinary* would live or die on the sexual chemistry, that crucial crackle between Celine and Robert.

Boyle and Macdonald's choice of cast was revealing. Hunter had given a dynamite performance in the Coen brothers' *Raising Arizona*, Dan Hedaya had starred as the betrayed spouse in their *Blood Simple*, Tony Shalhoub had cropped up in *Barton Fink*. Back in the early days, the director and producer had used *Blood Simple* as the template for their *Shallow Grave*. For their first American odyssey, the Coens would again point the way forward. Their off-kilter world-view and nimble mix of shock tactics and comedy have always had a big allure for the *Trainspotting* team. 'Yeah, we used a lot of the Coen brothers,' confesses Macdonald. 'I feed off other stuff deliberately. That's not unhealthy. You feed off everybody. I'm just a parasite. I love looting people and ideas.'

But there are other, older influences rattling around inside *A Life Less Ordinary*. Its shameless romanticism, reparcelled in glossy, postmodern fashion, sometimes calls to mind *One from the Heart*, Francis Coppola's florid musical folly from 1982. Its rat-a-tat dialogue and lovers-on-the-run plotline looks akin to the sophisticated screwball comedies of Hollywood's Golden Age. Before shooting began, Boyle significantly had his cast sit through a screening of Frank Capra's *It Happened One Night*, the vintage 1934 romantic-farce which made stars of Clark Gable and Claudette Colbert. Capra's stiletto-sharp sexual banter crops up all over the place in *A Life Less Ordinary*.

The film's last big influence was a movie with particular resonance for Andrew Macdonald. Powell and Pressburger's *A Matter of Life and Death* mixed gritty wartime reality with silk-spun fantasy in mapping out its tale of an RAF airman, Peter Carter (David Niven), caught in a ghostly limbo between Heaven and the real world. Having survived his crash, due in part to a celestial slip-up, Carter falls in love with an American woman (Kim Hunter). But Heaven wants to claim him and a trial is set in motion, with the winner to take the man's soul. Macdonald's grandfather, Emeric Pressburger, wrote the script and co-produced, while regular collaborator Michael Powell blended colour footage (for the Earth scenes) with lustrous black-and-white (for Heaven). Powell would later claim *A Matter of Life and Death* as his personal favourite of the films he made with Pressburger. (Macdonald's grandfather, though, plumped for the smaller, more idiosyncratic *A Canterbury Tale*.)

A Life Less Ordinary boasts obvious parallels with the Powell–Pressburger classic: the quirky depiction of Heaven; the spry blend of fantasy and reality; the cross-cultural love affair between a British chap and an American dame. In a sense the film serves as a kind of homage to the idiosyncratic genius of Powell and Pressburger, a lively repackaging of their style and concerns. *A Matter of Life and Death* was to become a key point of reference for the cast and crew of Boyle's film.

A Life Less Ordinary shot for fifty days in locations around Utah, stretching from late autumn into the winter of 1996. The makers had originally pencilled their film to play out in the state of North Carolina, but location scouts found the place lush, green and plagued by misty drizzles. The open expanse of the American Midwest better suited the road-movie aspect of Hodge's script and was more purely cinematic. 'We chose Utah because of the tremendous variety of landscape,' says Macdonald. 'It has harsh desert, beautiful mountains and buzzing city, all within a few hours' drive. And Utah is also one of the few states with good film technicians, so that was obviously very important to us.' Before the cameras rolled, Boyle set off on a ten-day tour of the area, travelling alone in a rental car, stopping off at roadhouses and spending nights in cheap motels. He explained:

> John and Andrew are not really into research. But I'm obsessed with it, not because I use it a lot, but because if you don't use it you cannot throw it away. Prior to that trip I had only been to the east and west coasts – neither of which is really "America". What struck me about the real American heartland is how young and optimistic it is. That pioneering spirit still exists, and I found it very romantic.

The director felt that the reconnaissance was crucial to him feeling comfortable in an unfamiliar setting: 'It's the first time that I've done a great deal of location shooting, because in Britain the landscape feels so small and claustrophobic. That's one reason our two previous films were composed almost entirely of interiors.'

The landscape is crucial to *A Life Less Ordinary*. Much of the film serves as a love letter to the American West; and since the audience's main point of identification throughout the film is a Scot abroad, the picture we get of this place comes from an outsider's stance, filtered through foreign eyes. At the same time, though, Boyle was determined not to fall back on a kind of tourist's view of the country, a photo album of American sights and sounds. With this in mind, he leaned heavily on the contribution of regular cinematography and design team Brian Tufano and Kave Quinn to perfect just the right look. Says Boyle:

> In Britain colours tend to be muddied and smudged so people won't notice them, and that's one of the things we've tried to rebel against. In preparing for our shoots we look at art: for *Trainspotting* we looked at lots of Francis Bacon and Edward Hopper, and for this one we've looked at paintings by Kitaj, photographs by Cartier-Bresson and Merry Alpern's book of voyeuristic photographs, *Dirty Windows*.

As a result, *A Life Less Ordinary* breaks from the deep textures that characterized the team's first two pictures. It has a hard, clean gloss to it, a look that's stylized to the 'nth degree.

Cast and crew set up base camp in Salt Lake City, with a hard-core contingent staying in a large rented house in the hills outside town. McGregor arrived with wife Eve and nine-month-old Clara in tow. As Boyle had predicted, he and Diaz struck up an immediate rapport. 'I'm always wary of meeting Hollywood actresses,' he confesses. 'I suppose it's a nasty prejudice but by and large my experiences with them haven't been the best. But Cameron is amazing, she really is. There's no bullshit to her, she's just out to enjoy herself. It made the atmosphere on-set really good.' At times, *A Life Less Ordinary*'s party atmosphere threatened to get out of hand. During the days' filming, McGregor and Diaz were separated by only the thinnest of connecting walls in the star trailer. When one of them was on the loo, the other could hear everything. All of which made any movie-star standoffishness seem ridiculous. Ewan and Cameron had no option but to get along – often to the exclusion of everyone around them. As Diaz recalled: 'They had to separate us. It was like, "You go in that corner and you go in the other corner, you can't play together any more. Put down the toys and go to work." '

The two stars needed to keep their spirits up. At times the shooting of *A Life Less Ordinary* sounds like the equivalent of National Service: a gang of buddies thrown together in the face of adversity. The problem was Utah, an archly conservative dry state a million miles away from the laid-back, anything-goes landscape of London or LA. For McGregor, accustomed to bar-hopping around the streets of Soho, the place proved a nightmare. 'It was without doubt the strangest fucking place I have ever been to in my life,' he says. 'It's like the land that time forgot.'

Even Salt Lake City, the area's most modern, populous setting, held few attractions. 'The whole town is built in this bowl where we don't have to think about the rest of the world,' Ewan remembers. 'You are absolutely safe from any normal people. It is built next to this huge, stagnant and stinking lake, which says rather a lot about the people who live there.' The headquarters of Mormonism, the city is a desert of shopping malls, stolid stone architecture and endless expanses of car-parking space.

'Everything is big and square,' explains Cameron Diaz. 'Because the Mormons have like six kids, they're thinking ahead about population. They know all these kids are going to be adults one day with their own children, so they've built all these stores that are, like, massive, with huge parking lots with enough parking space for everyone's mini vans.' McGregor identified another problem. 'It's full of religious nuts,' he says. 'They are out of control with that shit, let me tell you.'

On one chill afternoon in the middle of shooting, the actor took Eve and Clara out to shop at a local supermarket. Ewan was wearing a black woollen hat with the word 'PERVERT' (the clothing label) emblazoned across the front. 'I didn't think. I just put the hat on Clara's head because it was cold,' he remembered in an interview with *Elle* magazine. 'And the *looks*. I couldn't figure out why I was getting such death looks, and then I realized my ten-month-old baby's wearing a hat with 'pervert' written on it, and these people were like: "There's Satan! There's Satan out with his kid!" And then I made a big point of wearing it every time we went there.'

The 'pervert' label aside, McGregor felt resented by the townsfolk in general. With his casual gear, shaggy haircut and exotic foreign accent, he was viewed as something of a pariah by the decent God-fearing folk of Utah. 'You'd think that dragging a baby around would have made it easier, wouldn't you? But it exacerbated the whole situation. They seemed to hate the fact that here was this fucking scruff in sole charge of a child. They seemed to take it as a personal fucking insult.'

Andrew Macdonald puts on a braver face. For him, Salt Lake City was a crucial choice of location for the team's first American-set venture:

> It's a bit like working in Glasgow in some ways. We didn't want to work in Los Angeles. We're trying to avoid the industry towns and practice so we can make films the way we want to, not the way some union, or some studio, or some financiers want you to make them.

Their lead actor, though, remains unimpressed. 'Great skies, shit people,' he says. 'I was very, very glad to get out.'

Stuck in this backwater, *A Life Less Ordinary*'s cosmopolitan crew cast desperately around for entertainment. Since Utah was dry as dust, decent drinking holes proved hard to come by. The shooting schedule, too, was intense, so after a day's work, most of the cast and crew would just hang out and watch a video. On the nights before a day off from work, they would invariably hang out at Spanky's, a biker bar on the edge of the city. McGregor likens the experience to having a regular job: you work from nine to five and then go out and get slaughtered as a kind of *en masse* release, an escape from the drudge of reality. Diaz explains: 'He'd go home after the day, try to see Clara before she went to sleep. Get some good time in with the wife. I'd go home to my cat. Friday night it would be: "OK, Span-kys!."' McGregor would down some beers and shoot pool with the locals, or other members of the team. 'One night I hammered the fucking crap out of Danny,' Ewan recalls. 'They next day he said he couldn't believe it, because I was so drunk I could barely stand up, and was just talking nonsense, and yet I was hammering the balls in like I was fucking possessed.' On another occasion, he, Diaz and Danny Boyle had a go on the karaoke machine: a foretaste of *A Life Less Ordinary*'s flamboyant musical interlude (which was, incidentally, not shot in Spanky's). It was, McGregor says, like being a 'normal' person.

During working hours, cast and crew darted to and fro between a host of locations. The old Pony Express trail served for the film's desert interlude, while Robert and Celine's cabin was found in the canyons outside Salt Lake City. Where *Shallow Grave* and *Trainspotting* had pivoted around a scant series of settings, *A Life Less Ordinary* was constantly on the move. It was a long, tough, demanding shoot.

By the middle of December cast and crew were finished with Utah. Eve and

Clara returned to London while filming moved briefly to Malibu, where the scenes at the Neville mansion were shot. Finally, with his scenes in the can, McGregor darted across to Warner Brothers' Los Angeles studio. He had been offered a guest slot in a specially tailored episode of *ER*, America's number-one-rated TV drama. 'Total actor-ish self-indulgence, I know,' he says. 'But I've always been a big fan of the show and I just couldn't turn down the opportunity. And yeah, it was great fun.' For three days McGregor was on-set playing Duncan, a Scottish convenience-store robber who holds raven-headed Nurse Hathaway (Julianna Margoyles) hostage, then dies on the operating table at the episode's end. In acting terms, the part was hardly a stretch. The *ER* criminal is similar in tone to *A Life Less Ordinary*'s Robert: misguided, impetuous, basically decent. And while the surrounding story is darker than Boyle's feature, the *ER* episode could – with minor adjustments – have functioned perfectly well as a segment in the film. Duncan makes a few mistakes, digs himself into a hole and then tries to redeem himself. When he eventually dies (as we always knew he must), Nurse Hathaway weeps for him.

McGregor's *ER* stint was never going to rank up there with the actor's great performances. But it remains a professional job, neatly executed, with Ewan shifting convincingly from hardened villain to fightened, well-meaning youngster through the course of the fifty-five minute episode. Moreover, it netted its star an Emmy nomination and probably shoved his face in front of more viewers than *Trainspotting*, *Shallow Grave* or *Emma* ever could. When all is said and done, it was a shrewd move for McGregor.

In the meantime, there was trouble brewing back in London. With McGregor in LA, Clara came down with meningitis. The actor returned to his home in St John's Wood to find his daughter in hospital. McGregor couldn't help but feel a pang of guilt. 'Afterwards she was a wee bit weird with me,' he remembers. 'And on reflection I would rather not have gone.'

For McGregor, then, *A Life Less Ordinary* ended on a sour note. By Christmas, his work on the film was complete. In January, Boyle, Macdonald and editor Masahiro Hirakubo began piecing it all together.

● ● ● ● ●

But does *A Life Less Ordinary* actually work? Right from the start the production appeared beset by minor, niggly problems. There was Hodge's script, overhauled constantly and then switched around at the last moment. There were rumoured creative differences between Boyle and Macdonald and the bosses at Twentieth Century-Fox. During post-production, the team found themselves labouring to find a proper rhythm for the film. For while *Shallow Grave* had been kept deliberately simple, and *Trainspotting* worked off a perfectly honed script adapted from strong source material, *A Life Less Ordinary* proved a more wispy and mercurial affair. It was part romance, part slapstick, part thriller, part fantasy. It danced to its own music, and the tempo was constantly changing. When a rough cut was finally assembled, John Hodge remarked that the film was the strangest thing he'd seen since *Fire Walk with Me*, David Lynch's bewildering movie offshoot from his teasing TV series, *Twin Peaks*. When studio bosses went into a panic, Hodge hastened to put their minds at rest: 'But,' he insisted, '*I liked Fire Walk with Me*!'

The months leading up to its British release in October 1997 brought the almost audible sound of critics' daggers being sharpened. Those who had long nurtured the sneaking suspicion that *Shallow Grave* and *Trainspotting* were just that shade overrated prepared to put the boot in if film number three proved to be anything shy of flawless. In a way, Boyle, Macdonald, Hodge and McGregor had become victims of their own success. Everything they attempted *en masse* was bound to be thrust under a glaring spotlight of public attention. If they were to make a film five times as expensive as their previous one, surely it stood to reason that the finished product should be five times as impressive.

They were in an impossible position: damned if they did, damned if they didn't. If they had made another *Trainspotting*-type movie they would have been dismissed as one-trick ponies, but the sheer expectation-bucking difference of *A Life Less Ordinary* still caught a lot of people flat-footed. Just what manner of film was this? Ethereal fantasy rasped incongruously against gritty violence; Heaven with the real world; glum Scotland with brash, day-glo America. For many, its mix of ingredients was just a tad too rich and unprocessed.

By and large, the critics hated it. *The Times*'s Geoff Brown reckoned that: '*A Life Less Ordinary* may come festooned with fashionable names, a hip insouciance, intriguing conceits and sizeable audience expectations; but nothing much lies behind the bunting.' The *Observer*'s Philip French dubbed it: 'a display of isolated, narcissistic self-regard'. Richard Williams (replacing Derek Malcolm as the *Guardian*'s chief film critic) accused the film's makers of taking its audience too lightly and claimed that *A Life Less Ordinary* was 'more like a marketing exercise than a flesh-and-blood movie'. The *Evening Standard*'s Alexander Walker concluded that: 'Much of *A Life Less Ordinary* is the kind of mess that only gets worse as you try to make it better.' Tom Shone in the *Sunday Times* put the boot in still further: 'The whole film, in fact, has the feel of a small kid hoping to hold his own with his big brother's friends . . . Whether or not Ewan McGregor ever becomes a star,' he concluded, 'the first thing he must do is quit his current role as young mascot for the *Trainspotting* gang.'

Writing in the British edition of *Premiere*, Ryan Gilbey compared *A Life Less Ordinary* to *Be Here Now*, the Oasis album released two months prior to the film. One was a 'cocaine movie', the other a 'cocaine album'. The cocaine label was not a solid accusation, more a kind of shorthand for the moment when success turns to excess: the 'isolated narcissistic self-regard' which Philip French perceived. Where the previous works from both film-making team and rock band had been lean, hard and purposeful, *Premiere* reckoned these third offerings revealed nothing so much as an epic self-indulgence, a lack of perspective, a tell-tale absence of discipline. Both Oasis and the *Trainspotting* gang – fêted as the brightest British hopes in 1996 – had grown lazy and selfish, rampantly overestimating the public's tolerance for their antics. Almost all of the tracks on *Be Here Now* ran over seven minutes, their tight structures buried under a mound of jowly guitars and flabby, overrepeated refrains. Half-decent conceits were dragged out to inordinate length. Likewise, running longer than either *Shallow Grave* or *Trainspotting*, *A Life Less Ordinary* seemed to have overdressed itself and coated its inherent charm in an overload of sugar and superfluous ornaments. As a result, the album and film overstayed their welcome, stretching out like old elastic.

Ever the loyal Oasis fan, Ewan spotted the similarities, too. But he came at it from a different tack:

> It's our third film and it's like Oasis's new album. Number three. And the British press is bound to go for it. But I think that *Be Here Now* is actually a pretty fucking great album. And I love this movie, too. Maybe I'm too close to the finished film to see it properly, but I'm really very proud of it, particularly all the scenes between me and Cameron. The comedy of it all is just wonderful. I love the line

where Robert looks at her and says: "I'm doing the best I can under very diffi-cult circumstances." I think it's a really lovely film. We couldn't do another *Trainspotting*, because we've already done it. So this goes to the complete other extreme.

Even so, the buzz that had been there with *Trainspotting* was now notable only by its absence. In Britain, the film's performance was lacklustre, considering its wide release and the high-profile nature of its cast and crew. More importantly, this clearly American-targeted product conspicuously failed to make much imprint on the US box-office. In its first week it took a poor $2.7 million from a hefty 1,207 screens. The following week that tally had dropped by 53 per cent, and the week later by a worrying 78 per cent. Crucial word of mouth wasn't helping *A Life Less Ordinary*. Within a month it had vanished from most Stateside venues.

In fact, the picture is not as grim as the figures suggest. Its $12 million budget is a comparatively small outlay, a relatively easy sum to recoup. But it was not the big-money breakthrough that Macdonald had hoped. Meanwhile, running concurrently with *A Life Less Ordinary* came Robert Carlyle's star vehicle *The Full Monty*, playing to sell-out crowds and already on its way to becoming history's most successful British picture. All of which just goes to show the vagaries of the cinema-going public. On the face of it, *The Full Monty*, set in gloomy Sheffield and peopled by 'unsexy' unemployed types with regional dialects, should not have struck a chord in the foreign markets. On the face of it, *A Life Less Ordinary* – bright, escapist, with a pretty American star sharing the limelight – should have. But something had gone wrong with the mix. Some crucial ingredient was missing.

A Life Less Ordinary's reputation may well swell in the years to come. The film has enough rich and idiosyncratic aspects to justify a major reappraisal. Yet this is a strange, and not altogether successful creature. Its opening third is a peculiar mix of the tentative and the ingratiating. As a set-up, it is fumbled. As screwball comedy, it's worryingly charmless. Its ham-fisted humour, crude characters and bouncy soundtrack call to mind the synthetic teen comedies of the mid-eighties (*The Secret of My Success*, *Ferris Bueller's Day Off*). It is also not especially funny. Much of Hodge's comedy comes across as blunt and obvious, though McGregor may have to shoulder some of the blame here. The key scene where a spluttering Robert phones Neville with his ransom demand was apparently ad-libbed by the actor: it looks over-played and unsubtle. Moreover, the film comes saddled with too many in-jokes that presume audience familiarity with the men behind the action. We all know that Ewan McGregor is a big Oasis fan, so he gets to sing a raucous version of 'Round Are Way'. We all know that John Hodge wrote the script, so we have the characters engrossed in a trashy, Mills and Boon novel written by a certain 'Jennifer Hodge'. In the end, the nudge-nudge tone gets a touch irritating.

On the up-side, the film boasts some clusters of genuine silver-screen magic. There's that rousing karaoke scene that ignites a redneck bar, spiralling off wonderfully into pure fantasy. There's the tense stand-off in a deep, dark forest, REM's 'Leave' howling malevolently on the soundtrack. And there's the ending: giddy in its audacity and with a heart full of sweetness.

What's more, *A Life Less Ordinary* turns increasingly more assured as the plot progresses. The script, direction and acting seem to find their feet midway through, and begin to work in unison. The chemistry between McGregor and Diaz comes good, giving rise to a nice reversal of conventional sexual stereotypes in the film's faintly feminine, scream-queen hero and tough, go-getting heroine.

McGregor : Portrait of the artist as a Marlboro man. © David Sandison/Rex Features

Showbiz smiles : McGregor and Diaz face the cameras. © Hubert Boesl/Famous

Eye of the storm : McGregor with wife Eve Mavrakis. © Capital Pictures

Cannes' 96 : Macdonald, Welsh, Boyle, McGregor, Hodge. © Capital Pictures

Keeping his head in a world turned upside-down ... © Jim Cooper/Retna

Just two of McGregor's many faces.

Pensive ... © Armando Gallo/Retna

... and playful. © Rob Hann/Retna

White hat, black heart : As Meneer Chrome in *The Serpent's Kiss*. © Ronald Grant

The Serpent's Kiss : With co-star Greta Scaachi. © Ronald Grant

Silver jean machine : McGregor in Todd Haynes's *Velvet Goldmine*.

Velvet Goldmine : McGregor solo ...

... and with co-star Jonathon Rhys Meyers.

You're left with the suspicion that *A Life Less Ordinary* was the film that the team needed to get out of their system. It is a homage movie: the cinema equivalent of an album of cover versions. The picture tips its cap to Macdonald's grandfather with its reinvention of plot elements from *A Matter of Life and Death*, and acknowledges the impact the American landscape and American cinema have had on all concerned. *A Life Less Ordinary* is a classic valentine to all the influences of Boyle, Macdonald, Hodge and McGregor: charming in its way, but without the unity of vision, the passion to tell a story, that made *Trainspotting* so good. It trots out a roll call of inspirations (Golden Age Hollywood, Powell–Pressburger, the Coens), but there is little to anchor them. Ultimately, this fascinating folly is like a screwball comedy as rendered by Jeff Koons. It is visually flawless and bright as a button. But it is also chill and glassy at times – a flamboyant decoration as opposed to a full-blooded, organic story.

Of course, imitations are rarely as good as the genuine article. If the team was aiming to match the style and substance of their heroes, the Coen brothers, the finished product comes over as little more than karaoke mimicry. This was driven home harshly the following year with the release of the Coens' *The Big Lebowski*. The brothers' seventh movie shared *A Life Less Ordinary*'s kidnap plotline and mad romp through goofy Americana, but executed it with immeasurably more panache and consistency. Put the two films together and, in terms of wit, pacing and sheer entertainment value, *Lebowski* wins hands down.

Nonetheless, *A Life Less Ordinary* is a brave film, frequently charming, and an ambitious attempt by its makers to distance themselves from the *Trainspotting* label. In hindsight, perhaps, it could never hope to match the impact of its predecessor. 'Apart from anything else,' points out Andrew Macdonald, 'it doesn't have the same sociological and cultural joining at the hip.' Rather than a startling x-ray on British culture, then, the team's difficult number three is a more playful, personal affair, an extravagant flight of fantasy. Boyle reckons it will be seen as 'our *New York, New York*', comparing it to Martin Scorsese's unloved 1977 romance which broke joltingly away from the style of *Mean Streets* and *Taxi Driver*. It is up to history to judge *A Life Less Ordinary*. Maybe film number three will come to be seen as a blip, a disaster or a much-maligned masterpiece: an ahead-of-its-time classic, a kitsch daintee for the next millennium.

END OF THE CENTURY

10. END OF THE CENTURY

Ewan McGregor's work rate calls to mind the latter stages of some study in quantum mechanics. As he gets older, he's speeding up. 'People are always telling me I should slow down,' he says. 'But I think: "Why? For what?" I have', he confesses, 'a trouble saying no.' In a sense, though, McGregor is merely keeping pace with the accelerating curve of British film production as a whole. In 1995, there were 78 homegrown pictures produced; in 1996 (the year of *Trainspotting*'s release) there were 128. Actor and industry have become inextricably bound up. The one impacts on the other.

So McGregor moves from one film set to another, slipping through a variety of artistic hoops, an array of different challenges. As the century draws to its close he has evolved into a kind of one-man acting enterprise. A firm commitment from McGregor is enough to green-light almost any project.

Even given the below-par performance of *A Life Less Ordinary*, Ewan McGregor came out of 1997 with his reputation further enhanced. While public and critics seemed lukewarm to the film as a whole, McGregor's performance – a mini-masterwork of squawking, emasculated cuteness – appeared to give little cause for concern. Moreover, *A Life Less Ordinary*'s Robert signalled a virtuoso change of pace from his tight, cynical Renton. And even if he had slipped up, no matter. There was still a clutch of other films in the can, lined up and ready for release. McGregor has dipped a toe into the American film industry with *Nightwatch* and embarked on another art-house, jigsaw-puzzle of a picture with his turn as a lusty landscape gardener in Philippe Rousselot's *The Serpent's Kiss*.

More significant is his co-starring role in Todd Haynes's *Velvet Goldmine*, which was shot in and around London through the spring of 1997. For Haynes is arguably the most vital and intriguing film-maker to come out of the US indie scene in years. Based in New York, he first came to attention with the pointed, provocative *Superstar*, an off-kilter biopic of singer Karen Carpenter, played out with a cast of plastic Barbie dolls. More mainstream interest followed with *Safe*, a trippy, unsettling study of environmental illness starring Julianne Moore as a brittle LA housewife laid low by an intangible environmental illness. Deftly directed and delicately unnerving, *Safe* cropped up on many end-of-year round-ups as the best film of 1996.

Those tracing Ewan McGregor's rock-star parallels should have a field day with *Velvet Goldmine*. The actors plays peroxide rocker Curt Wild, a piece of 'Michigan trailer-trash' who roars his way through early Iggy Pop numbers ('TV Eye', 'Gimme Danger') and shakes glitter onto his sweaty torso. 'I played the Brixton Academy in front of about 300 extras and went mad,' McGregor remembers. 'I ended up with my silver jeans around my ankles, butt naked. It was fantastic.'

Although nominally relegated to a supporting role, McGregor towers head and shoulders above the rest of *Velvet Goldmine*'s cast (which includes comic Eddie Izzard as a megalomaniac manager and Jonathan Rhys Meyers as Bowie surrogate Brian Slade). His performance is assured and charismatic within the limits of his allotted screen time, although a dodgy American accent (turning all Perthshire around the corners) does support Boyle and Macdonald's decision to play him as a Scot in *A Life Less Ordinary*.

The film itself is a fascinating and elusive thing. During its final stages, rumours pointed to major problems in the editing suite and the final product does indeed have a sprawling and ill-disciplined feel to it, as though three or four separate pictures have somehow been shoehorned together. *Velvet Goldmine* spins the *Citizen Kane*-style tale of missing glam rocker Brian Slade; gone undercover after a publicity stunt goes awry and hounded ten years later by a British journalist (Christian Bale) in New York. The film spotlights the glam-rock scene, in particular, and youth trends in general, and waxes lyrical, and at some length, on the strains of homosexuality running throughout British culture (from Oscar Wilde to vaudeville via rock 'n' roll androgyny). At times its myriad ambitions don't quite gel, yet Haynes's film remains both a stunning evocation of a bygone age (ostrich-plumed flamboyance over-running the drab seventies suburbs) plus a complex, layered thesis on how pop culture is manufactured; the means by which the nation's youth re-invent themselves and seek to take charge of their own destinies. Originally a nondescript kid from Birmingham, Slade undergoes a metamorphosis that is part fantasy, part truth, part bullshit. 'He was like nothing I'd ever seen before,' reminisces his ex-manager, 'and in the end like nothing he appeared. He was walking arm in arm with a lie.'

More so than any previous McGregor film, *Velvet Godlmine* is anchored by its music. Fittingly, the film was executive produced by REM frontman Michael Stipe, while its soundtrack makes room for the likes of such past and present luminaries as T-Rex, Pulp, Lou Reed, Thom Yorke, Roxy Music and Grant Lee

Buffalo. When all is said and done, *Velvet Goldmine* ranks as a vibrant addition to the McGregor CV.

But during the making of Todd Haynes's film there was an even bigger project looming on the horizon. Immediately before shooting began, Ewan McGregor attended a hush-hush meeting with George Lucas, who, since shooting the original *Star Wars* in 1977, had abandoned direction in favour of the business end of the film industry. Yet Lucas, it transpired, was planning a return to the director's seat. The three *Star Wars* films (*Star Wars*, 1980's *The Empire Strikes Back* and 1983's *Return of the Jedi*) had always been intended as just the opening salvoes of an epic nine-film series, and two decades on from the original instalment, Lucas felt ready to begin work on chapter four. With the working title of *Balance of the Force*, this was to be a prequel not a sequel.

Balance of the Force retraces its steps to the days before Luke Skywalker and Princess Leia, and probes at the origins of the 'Force', that Zen-like energy source that the protagonists tap into. A hunt was on to find a young British actor to play the youthful Ben Obi-Wan Kenobi, the Jedi knight played by Sir Alec Guinness in the original movie. Kenneth Branagh was one possibility; Ewan McGregor another.

'I met the casting director about a year and a half or two years ago,' McGregor remarked in the spring of 1998. 'Then a year later, almost to the day, I went back and met her again. And then I met George and Rick McCollum, who's a producer. Then I screen-tested with Liam Neeson. Then I got offered the job.' His fee for the film is a rumoured £4 million, together with a percentage of the picture's eventual gross.

The *Star Wars* shoot is, however, shrouded in secrecy. Upon learning that he had won the part, McGregor was impelled to sign a confidentiality agreement promising to reveal no details of the plot, or even the mechanics of the shoot. Some say that Lucas even ordered phoney scripts to be 'leaked' into circulation in an attempt to muddy the waters still further. All of which has turned the long-awaited *Star Wars* prequel into the cinema equivalent of a Cold War battle-plan: wreathed in impenetrable code and known only to the select few. 'It's very unusual, but it's true!' McGregor insists:

> The second anything's divulged it's straight on to the Internet. And also I think George gets sued all the time. People send him scripts that he won't open and sends back. But then he gets sued because he's rich. I think he spends weeks in court every year fending off these court cases.

On returning to his *Velvet Goldmine* day job, the actor found himself forced to bite his tongue.

> I'd just heard I'd got the part and I was walking around with this fucking big stupid grin on my face. I wanted to leap up and down but I was sworn to secrecy. Added to that was the fact that I had to concentrate on my role. That day seemed to last about four fucking weeks.

Balance of the Force shot in the deserts of Tunisia and in the confines of London's Leavesden Studios during the summer of 1997. Inevitably wisps of rumour and hearsay escaped from its closed set. *Balance of the Force*, it transpires, traces the roots of the war between the Republic and the Empire. *Schindler's List* star Liam Neeson plays a veteran Jedi knight who serves as a mentor for the young Obi-Wan. In turn, Obi-Wan saves the life of child scamp Annakin (played by ten-year-old Jake Lloyd) who grows up into a Jedi knight ally. Together Annakin and Obi-Wan battle the dark forces of the Force on a waterlogged planet.

Balance of the Force is itself only the first instalment in a three-film set of prequels, all of which McGregor is signed up for. Future films promise to see Annakin and Obi-Wan quarrel (over a woman, apparently) and the younger man swings towards evil. He will eventually become Darth Vader: leader of the Empire and father of Luke Skywalker.

The cast-list is impressive. Alongside McGregor and Neeson, *Balance of the Force* makes room for Terence Stamp, Natalie Portman, Brian Blessed, Adrian Dunbar and Samuel L Jackson. Meantime, back from the first films comes old-hand Kenny Baker, once again ensconced in the shell of R2D2. 'I went home one day and my wife was sitting with a lot of her mates,' McGregor says, 'and I go, "I worked with R2D2 today," and they all looked at me and went, "Who?" I guess it's a boy's thing. The chicks just don't get it.'

In fact, the whole experience became something of a fantasy-made-flesh for McGregor. The film he had seen as a callow infant was now a part of his day-to-day routine. He had become a piece of its history: a star actor in the most successful series in cinema history. 'Yeah, every day I found myself having a *Star Wars* moment,' he says. 'It's like reliving your childhood in this exaggerated, out-of-proportion way. Having my own light sabre took a bit of getting used to.'

Although wary of signing up to conventional Hollywood blockbusters, McGregor had no problem committing to the Lucas project. 'I don't think there's a comparison really,' he says. 'I don't see *Star Wars* as being of or about Hollywood, to be honest. I think it pretty much exists in a world of its own.' Nonetheless, the Lucas film pushes its star into a whole different league; potentially nudging him up towards the pantheon of the world's biggest box-office performers. *Balance of the Force* is less a straightforward film than a kind of global phenomenon, a marketing exercise to rank among the greats. Immediately after filming, McGregor was given a brochure of merchandise tie-ins to pick out a few free gifts for Clara. 'The brochure was about three inches thick! There were T-shirts, toy spaceships, light sabres, action-men. And yes, it is very fucking weird to be a part of that.'

On a more artistic level, too, the film had its surprises. Lucas's comeback was shot on a scale far exceeding anything that McGregor had previously experienced. Before shooting began, the actor looked over the previous films; studying Alec Guinness's body movements and vocal intonations. It was a struggle, he admitted, to find an accurate impersonation of Guinness that avoided being a kind of karaoke mimicry, while at the same time playing Obi-Wan as a young man: a salad of Guinness's and McGregor's respective character traits.

On set, though, there were times when such carefully structured techniques threatened to be overwhelmed by a flurry of sci-fi paraphernalia. Lucas's pioneering Industrial Light and Magic special-effects factory apparently promise an average of thirteen visual effects in each scene: a treasure trove of computer-generated characters and backdrops. All of which limits the scope for flesh-and-blood acting. Says McGregor:

Making a film like *Star Wars* was unique for me. With other films you essentially know exactly what you're doing. You walk on to the set and play the scene with the other actors. And then you see it in the finished movie. On *Star Wars* there were times when I had not the faintest idea what was going on. It was all that blue-screen bullshit. You're acting a scene standing in this empty studio space, often acting to nothing, just thrashing about in space. Then the scene is taken away and all kinds of stuff is done to it, and then it's inserted into the movie, completely altered. There was a little bit of that with Greenaway on *The Pillow Book*, but this was just a totally different process. It's quite hard to keep your mind on the acting when all the props are taken away from you. But hopefully I've learned a lot from it.

McGregor completed the principal photography in September 1997, but had to dash across to the United States at the start of 1998 for a few quick re-shoots. The film itself is not scheduled for release until the following summer. The lead actor, though, predicts it is more likely to be even later than that.

> I think right now it's safe to say Christmas 1999, right before the end of the millennium. Good timing, I think. There's eighteen months of post-production. There were two years of pre-production and three and a half months of shooting. That shows you how important the acting is.

But if *Balance of the Force* left McGregor feeling understretched as an actor, he has been quick to make amends. After the Lucas shoot he was immediately off on another round of more low-budget, performance-driven enterprises: *The Eye of the Beholder, Rogue Trader* and *The Rise and Fall of Little Voice*. The first of these is a Canadian-set psychological thriller directed by Australian Stephan Elliott (of *Priscilla, Queen of the Desert* fame) and co-starring Ashley Judd and *Beverly Hills 90210* graduate Jason Priestley. *The Rise and Fall of Little Voice* sees McGregor playing a second-string role to Michael Caine and Jane Horrocks, who reprises her stage role as a silver-screen-obsessed mimic in the north of England. The film was shot in Scarborough and reunites Ewan with Mark Herman, who directed him to such good effect in *Brassed Off*.

On the face of it, *Rogue Trader* looks a classic example of the way cinema inherently glamorizes a fact-based source, warping it out of all proportion. In it,

McGregor portrays financial whizz-kid Nick Leeson, the reviled scamster whose cavalier antics in the Far East futures market helped run up the £800-million debt which broke Barings Bank. James Dearden's production, culled from Leeson's tell-all autobiography, shifts the balance more in the villain's favour. In a sense, *Rogue Trader* becomes an exposé of the British class system, with a working-class tearaway bashing out a niche in the old-boy City of London, where he helps turn Barings from a tweedy merchant bank into a hustling trading house, and then gets tossed to the lions when it all goes wrong. 'It's a story about money,' Dearden explains of the film. 'It's a real slice of history and it symbolizes a turning point, when the Barings of this world were finally consigned to history.' Looking startlingly young in short back and sides and a pristine white shirt, McGregor plays Leeson as a kind of British variant on Charlie Sheen's role in *Wall Street*: the upwardly mobile hotshot who comes a cropper in the cut-throat world of international finance.

Rogue Trader was shot in Singapore and in a monetary exchange mocked up at Pinewood Studios through the early months of 1998. Co-starring alongside McGregor are character actor John Standing (as Peter Barings) and Anna Friel (as Lisa Leeson), who became the fodder for much tabloid speculation over whether she and McGregor were conducting an off-set affair. A brief mouth-to-mouth kiss, snapped by a keen-eyed member of the paparazzi added further fuel to the fire.

Such films continue to test McGregor and to tone up his acting muscles. 'It's important for me to keep going,' he explains. 'I've always been very driven, but it's an artistic drive as opposed to the whole celebrity bullshit.' He has yet, he feels, to hit his peak as an actor. 'No way is something like *Star Wars* the ultimate acting experience, and that's what I'm always striving for. It's like being a surfer,' he says, harping back to his stint on the unloved *Blue Juice*. 'I'm travel-ling the world trying to find the perfect wave.'

● ● ● ● ●

In the meantime, McGregor's fledgling Natural Nylon production arm continues to nurture projects of its own. Topping the list is *Nora*, a James Joyce biopic, rescued by the company after it looked to be floundering. Other scripts in the pipeline include a biography of Beatles manager Brian Epstein, an adaptation of the Iain Banks book *The Bridge* and a story about the Hellfire Club, a crop of young eighteenth-century rakes who ran amok through London town. McGregor is pencilled in to star, along with Natural Nylon cohorts Sean Pertwee, Jude Law and Jonny Lee Miller. 'Yeah, we can relate to the Hellfire Club,' muses McGregor. 'They were our kind of people.'

Natural Nylon points the possible way forward for Ewan McGregor – a close-knit group of actors taking charge of their own destinies and fashioning their own tailor-made projects. Moreover, the fact that Natural Nylon aims to remain in London, backing British films, looks a heartening sign for home-grown film production. Ewan, Miller and Law may occasionally flirt with Hollywood and snatch its easy money, but, unlike the generation of actors immediately preced-ing them (Tim Roth, Gary Oldman), they remain firmly committed to Britain as their regular workplace. Needless to say, the industry is stronger with them around.

But Natural Nylon is in its early days. McGregor's main collaboration is still with the team that made him a star. He is determined that this will continue to be the case:

Out of all my work as an actor, it's the films I've done with Danny, Andrew and John that I'm most proud of. Those are the ones that really matter. When we're not working we don't hang out together much. But I always know that they're there. I love the fact that I've been involved in all three of their films. And I would have a real problem if they were making a movie and decided that they didn't need me to work on it. But I know it's bound to happen one day.

Andrew Macdonald is not so sure. Once again he looks to the work of Powell and Pressburger for his inspiration.

One lesson I learned from my grandfather's and Michael's work is that they had this core group of people they worked with over and over. As for Ewan, how many [films] has De Niro done with Scorsese? Or Mastroianni with Fellini? Danny and Ewan still have a way to go, haven't they?

In the meantime, Boyle and Macdonald were also forging ahead with schemes of their own. Just prior to *A Life Less Ordinary*, they took time out from the front line of film production to executive-produce Kevin Allen's writing and directing debut *Twin Town*. Allen had already enjoyed a spry, one-word cameo in *Trainspotting*, alongside his elder brother Keith, but *Twin Town* (initially to be titled *Pretty Shitty City*) heralded a return to his Welsh roots. This aggressively hyped revenge comedy turned sleepy Swansea into a kind of petty-crime Disneyland and worked as an ongoing, stylized farce. With its iconic imagery, voguish stars and natty drug accoutrements, *Twin Town* appeared desperately to want to be adopted as 1997's *Trainspotting*. The trouble was that it conspicuously lacked that movie's edge, heart or insight. This was a coldly marketed, identikit 'youth picture', its dialogue heaving with pop-culture references and peppered all over the place with the 'F-word' ('ex-fucking-actly'; 'Al Pa-fucking-cino'). Box-offce business was adequate but the film failed to strike any chord with the culture at large.

Twin Town was released in Britain five months before *A Life Less Ordinary*, which the makers confidently expected would be their beach-head into the American market. The fact that it failed to be the hoped-for crossover hit made 1997 something less than a vintage year for the *Trainspotting* team. But film-makers wither and die if they don't move forward and try something new. At the very least, *A Life Less Ordinary* revealed a new variety in Boyle, Macdonald and Hodge, a hitherto unseen side of their talents. Plus the film eventually crawled into profit which, in studio terms, is the bottom line.

For their fourth project, the team look to be returning to the *Trainspotting* formula: adapting a zeitgeist British novel for the screen. In 1997 Macdonald snapped up the rights for Alex Garland's *The Beach*, a *Lord of the Flies*-type story about the hippy trail in Thailand. While not as compelling source material as the Welsh book, twenty-seven-year-old Garland's debut tale still became a critical hit and a commercial bestseller. Moreover, *The Beach* rustles up a dark and playful take on a side of life – the drifting, backpacker set – rarely before detailed on page or screen. Also, adds the ever-savvy Macdonald, this youth-centred novel has all the right elements for the global market. 'A big thing is the international element,' he points out. 'It's a beach, so no identifiable country, with characters from all over the place.' Reassuringly, Ewan McGregor is already pencilled in to take the starring role.

Also in the pipeline is an adaptation of James Hawes's Brit gangster book *A White Merc with Fins*. Then there is *Alien Love Triangle*, an idiosyncratic portmanteau picture to be produced by Figment Films with Danny Boyle helming one of its three segments. All of which should see Figment safely through to the twenty-first century.

It's safe to assume that whatever Boyle, Macdonald and Hodge try next is guaranteed to grab widespread attention. *Shallow Grave* was a dynamite calling card; *Trainspotting* earned them a place in cinema history; *A Life Less Ordinary* showed that they have other strings to their bow. Taken as a whole, this trinity of movies has shoved the team into the pole position of home-grown film production. They have become the symbol of a wider resurgence in British cinema and the key reference point to deeper trends: the leaders of a bright new scene.

Away from the immediate Figment orbit, the signs are encouraging, with a gathering swell in domestic film production. Obviously Boyle, Macdonald and Hodge can't claim the credit for such a leap, but the *Shallow Grave/Trainspotting* factor surely played a part. Both films demonstrated that British-made pictures in a modern-day British setting could find a mass mainstream audience. They triggered a new optimism among both film-makers and film backers, a can-do climate noticeably at odds with the insular conservatism that typified the late eighties and early nineties.

Even so, the stellar performance of *Trainspotting* remains something of an anomaly. Its pure-blood British pedigree is not matched by the other success stories which surround it. Mike Leigh's Cannes award-winning *Secrets and Lies* was part-funded by France. The multi-Oscar-winning *The English Patient*, though directed by an Englishman (Anthony Minghella), starring two English actors (Ralph Fiennes and Kristin Scott Thomas) and adapted from an English novel, was still essentially a Hollywood product. Even the feel-good Sheffield comedy *The Full Monty*, though brightly trumpeted as history's most successful British picture, was awash with American money.

All of which makes *Trainspotting* the template for the burgeoning British film scene, a self-sustaining industry with major export potential. At present the signs are promising. Since 1996 the channelling of National Lottery funds into domestic film production has further eased the burden of cobbling together minor budgets in a piecemeal fashion. By the end of 1997 the scheme had its first genuine hit. Stefan Schwartz's *Shooting Fish*, a breezy, Ealing-style comedy about London con-artists, made a robust showing at the European box-office and allowed its makers to make a prompt repayment of their million-pound lottery-fund loan.

But the present British cinema scene is a fragile, air-bubble entity. Nobody is quite sure precisely how healthy it is. Is this a genuine grass-roots resurgence or a buoyant blip on an otherwise downward curve? Sceptics would claim that there was a similar level of optimism in the early eighties, and that it all proved to be a false dawn. More worryingly, it is possible to compare the patchy performance of *A Life Less Ordinary* to the abrupt dimming of the Brit-pop music scene, reflected in lacklustre sales of the latest albums from Pulp, Sleeper, Black Grape and Portishead. Concerned with the wobbly history of British film, critics caution against opportunism; of pump-priming a still relatively puny industry; of flooding the market with a proliferation of ill-conceived pictures without the audience to sustain them. Despite assurances, there remains only a slender home audience for native British pictures. Hollywood blockbusters still dominate the end-of-year charts.

Nonetheless there remains a pervading sense of optimism throughout all areas of the British arts landscape. Call it a new spirit of independence; a budding confidence; a do-it-yourself ethos; a creative upswing; a certain spontaneity. Whatever it is, Danny Boyle has no doubt of its existence:

> It only used to be theatrical people or BBC people who got to make films in Britain. Films always had to be properly financed and everyone was always complaining how hard it was to get the money you needed. In America, you had

people like Spike Lee or the guy who made *Clerks* [Kevin Smith] who just basically made their films and then audiences went to see them. But that never happened here, not one film in Britain ever did that. The closest we'd get to that ideal would be *Leon the Pig Farmer*.

Now we have *Trainspotting*, *Shooting Fish* and *TwentyFourSeven*, 1998's acclaimed debut feature from twenty-five-year-old Midlands dole kid Shane Meadows. The times they are a-changing.

● ● ● ● ●

If this scattered, heterogeneous scene requires a symbol, Ewan Gordon McGregor fits the bill. In these current, re-energized days he stands out as a child of his time. His fortunes mirror Britain's fortunes; his career parallels that of the industry he inhabits. On the face of it, his has been a strange and giddy trip. McGregor's route has taken him from a bungalow in Perthshire to a million-pound home in St John's Wood; from rep theatre to big-money cinema; from city-street busking to the Brixton Academy. No doubt success has changed him. 'Of course it's changed him,' says *Shallow Grave* co-star Kerry Fox. 'It's made him more happy!' Yet, to all intents and purposes, he looks to have come through the whole stardom madness remarkably unscathed. At the bottom line, there is a bedrock constancy to Ewan McGregor, a symmetry and simplicity to his course through life. As a six-year-old he left his home in Crieff to see his Uncle Denis in George Lucas's *Star Wars*. Twenty years on he is starring in the follow-up. The wheel has spun back to the point where it began. In a strange, roundabout way, Ewan McGregor has come full circle. In the process, everything around him has changed beyond all recognition.

FILMOGRAPHY

Being Human (UK/US: 1993)

Director: Bill Forsyth

Robin Williams, John Turturro, Anna Galiena, Vincent D'Onofrio

Family Style (UK: 1994)

Director: Justin Chadwick

Ewan McGregor, Amelia Curtis

Shallow Grave (UK: 1994)

Director: Danny Boyle

Christopher Eccleston, Kerry Fox, Ewan McGregor, Keith Allen

Blue Juice (UK: 1995)

Director: Carl Prechnezer

Sean Pertwee, Catherine Zeta-Jones, Ewan McGregor

Trainspotting (UK: 1995)

Director: Danny Boyle

Ewan McGregor, Robert Carlyle, Ewan Bremner, Jonny Lee Miller

Emma (UK/US: 1996)

Director: Doug McGrath

Gwyneth Paltrow, Jeremy Northam, Greta Scaachi, Ewan McGregor

Brassed Off (UK: 1996)

Director: Mark Herman

Pete Postlethwaite, Stephen Tompkinson, Ewan McGregor, Tara Fitzgerald

The Pillow Book (UK: 1996)

Director: Peter Greenaway

Vivian Wu, Ewan McGregor

A Life Less Ordinary (UK: 1997)

Director: Danny Boyle

Ewan McGregor, Cameron Diaz, Ian Holm, Holly Hunter

Nightwatch (US: 1997)

Director: Ole Bornedal

Ewan McGregor, Patricia Arquette, Nick Nolte

The Serpent's Kiss (UK: 1997)

Director: Philippe Rousselot

Ewan McGregor, Greta Scaachi, Pete Postlethwaite, Richard E Grant

Velvet Goldmine (UK: 1998)

Director: Todd Haynes

Ewan McGregor, Jonathan Rhys Meyers, Christian Bale, Toni Collette

FILMOGRAPHY

Rogue Trader (UK: 1998)

Director: James Dearden

Ewan McGregor, Anna Friel, John Standing

The Rise and Fall of Little Voice (UK: 1998)

Director: Mark Herman

Jane Horrocks, Michael Caine, Ewan McGregor

Eye of The Beholder (US/Can: 1999)

Director: Stephan Elliot

Ashley Judd, Ewan McGregor, Jason Priestley

Star Wars: Balance of The Force (US: 1999)

Director: George Lucas

Ewan McGregor, Liam Neeson, Natalie Portman

TELEVISION

Lipstick on Your Collar (UK: 1993)

Director: Renny Rye

Giles Thomas, Ewan McGregor, Louise Germaine, Kymberly Huffman

Scarlet and Black (UK: 1993)

Director: Ben Bolt

Ewan McGregor, Rachel Weisz

Doggin' Around (UK: 1994)

Director: Otto Plaschkes

Elliot Gould, Geraldine James, Ewan McGregor

Kavanagh QC: Nothing but The Truth (UK: 1995)

Director: Colin Cregg

John Thaw, Ewan McGregor

ER: The Long Way Around (US: 1997)

Director: Christopher Chulack

Julianna Margulies, Ewan McGregor, George Clooney

SOME OTHER FILM TITLES AVAILABLE FROM ANDRÉ DEUTSCH

Please address orders to:

Littlehampton Book Services

14 Eldon Way

Lineside Estate

Littlehampton

West Sussex

BN17 7HE

Tel: 01903 721596

Fax: 01903 730914

Email: 100067.1613@compuserve.com

DAVID LEAN

By Stephen M Silverman

This stunning tribute to one of the world's finest film directors represents the first time that the reticent director of *Brief Encounter, Great Expectations, The Bridge on the River Kwai, Lawrence of Arabia* and *Doctor Zhivago*, gave his full consent and co-operation to a project documenting his life and work. The result is a book as spectacular as his critically acclaimed films.

Lean tells his story with honesty and verve, assisted by the authoritative viewpoints of Alec Guinness, Katharine Hepburn, Sarah Miles, John Mills, Michael Powell and Omar Sharif. With numerous pictures and photos, some taken from the private archives of Katharine Hepburn, as well as Lean himself, no cinema lover should miss out on this stunning tribute to one of the silver screen's most influential figures.

ISBN 0 233 98464 X
£25 HB
216pp with colour and black and white photos throughout
285 x 225mm

FRENCHY'S GREASE SCRAPBOOK

By Didi Conn

Grease, the movie, has achieved true cult status. The highest grossing film and video of all time and a sell-out West End musical, it's taken on a whole new relevance for the 1990s, and this is the book to celebrate it!

Didi Conn played Frenchy, the lovable beauty school dropout, and she's our tour guide in this photo journey through the life and times of *Grease*. Containing never-before-revealed stories and personal behind-the-scenes photos from the cast and crew, *Frenchy's Grease Scrapbook* will take you into the midst of auditions, reveal the frenetic shooting schedule and the candid moments between takes, and reflect upon the incredible impact that the film had upon both its cast and its audiences.

Including contributions from John Travolta, Olivia Newton John, Stockard Channing and Jeff Conaway, *Frenchy's Grease Scrapbook* is the heavenly must-have for 'hopelessly devoted' Grease fans everywhere!

ISBN 0 233 99463 7
£8.99 PB
192pp with 200 colour and black and white photos
276 x 218mm

THE EMPIRE FILM QUIZ BOOK

By the Empire staff

The Empire Film Quiz Book is the ultimate test of your movie knowledge. Defying the limits of film knowledge, the quizzes swoop from animation to Altman, *Jaws* to *Star Wars*, encompassing cult movies and dud movies, opening lines and tag lines.

Taking its lead form the magazine's funny, quirky and original monthly quiz, and illustrated with dozens of brilliant photographs, this is the ideal book for everyone who likes the pink Trivial Pursuits questions best.

ISBN 0 233 99234 0
£9.99 PB
112pp with colour and black and white photos
246 x 189mm

CHAMELEON

THE FINEST YEARS
BRITISH CINEMA OF THE 1940s

By Charles Drazin

The Finest Years offers a new depth of understanding to a previously neglected area of popular culture, and recaptures the spirit of the golden age of British cinema.

In this illuminating and insightful tour de force, Charles Drazin considers a crucial epoch of British cinema, providing fascinating insights into the film makers' characters, circumstances and aspirations.

ISBN 0 233 98985 4
£17.99 HB
288pp with 16pp of black and white photos
234 x 156mm

RALPH FIENNES: THE BIOGRAPHY

By York Membery

Ralph Fiennes has been acclaimed as the greatest actor of his time. As desired as Brando, as private as Alec Guinness and as English as David Niven. He has a screen presence and theatrical *tour de force* that has not been seen since Olivier.

Mysterious and complex, the star of *Schindler's List* and *The English Patient* has attempted to shield his private life and true self from the public. Now read behind the eyes – the unauthorised life of Ralph Fiennes.

ISBN 0 233 99290 1

£9.99 PB

224pp with 16pp of colour and black and white photos

234 x 156mm